Great

Great Britain

Our Road to Disaster

Brian Stanyer

Copyright © 2024 by Brian Stanyer.

Library of Congress Control Number:		2024916142
ISBN:	Hardcover	978-1-6698-9102-4
	Softcover	978-1-6698-9103-1
	eBook	978-1-6698-9101-7

All rights reserved. No part of this book may be reproduced or transmitted in any form or by any means, electronic or mechanical, including photocopying, recording, or by any information storage and retrieval system, without permission in writing from the copyright owner.

Any people depicted in stock imagery provided by Getty Images are models, and such images are being used for illustrative purposes only.
Certain stock imagery © Getty Images.

Print information available on the last page.

Rev. date: 08/12/2024

To order additional copies of this book, contact:
Xlibris
UK TFN: 0800 0148620 (Toll Free inside the UK)
UK Local: (02) 0369 56328 (+44 20 3695 6328 from outside the UK)
www.Xlibrispublishing.co.uk
Orders@Xlibrispublishing.co.uk

In Britain there is a malaise and listlessness. You can detect it in the streets and workplaces, in the schools and universities, in the hospitals, public houses and the homes.

We need inspiration, purpose and direction because we have lost our way, our confidence, our determination, our vision and hunger.

We need a Wellington or a Churchill. Where are you?

CONTENTS

Chapter 1   Introduction 1
Chapter 2   Britain's Major Current Problems..................9
Chapter 3   Immigration and UK Population 17
Chapter 4   Political Systems of Government................23
Chapter 5   The Present Government Structure.............26
Chapter 6   Local Government..37
Chapter 7   Referenda..45
Chapter 8   Taxation 47
Chapter 9   About People. 49
Chapter 10 Reconsidering The Country's Problems 62
Chapter 11 Action that We Need to Take 66
Chapter 12 Public Services 79
Chapter 13 Health Services...89
Chapter 14 Other matters to consider. 92
Chapter 15 Religious Matters....................................... 101
Chapter 16 Unemployment, Training and Retraining ..109
Chapter 17 Environmental Issues. 117
Chapter 18 The final summary of what I believe we need to do. .. 119

CHAPTER 1

Introduction

I WAS BORN IN Northern England in a small Cheshire village. As far as I can trace, all my ancestors for many generations were British born and my family and I have a love for this country, its people, and our way of life.

I'm writing this short book because I have a desperate fear for our future and that we are going to leave, for our descendants, a community which is desperately indebted, poorly governed and controlled, with poverty and uncertainty for future generations and a danger of civil conflict.

I am now an old man and will be long gone before most of my fears are realized but unless we wake up soon our future is dire. We in some ways may already be too late.

This book may seem to many of you to be disjointed, lacking organisation, somewhat muddled and repetitive. I plead guilty to all of these and ask your tolerance and understanding because there is no plot for what I want to say, but a host of problems the solutions for which are many, varied and always difficult. I'm sure in parts it is somewhat inaccurate and you may have better information, but I want to see a country which is safe and secure with greater equality of opportunity and fairness for all citizens.

I suppose I'm writing this for Labour Party members but many of them will not like it because they believe in nationally controlled businesses, high taxation and state-run public services many of which can be harmful. We have had this policy for many years, even with

Conservative Governments, and it has not solved the problems of inequality and poverty and left us with enormous debt. I want to rethink how we can achieve our objectives and design new systems which create a better future.

We have now allowed the development of a multiracial and multicultural society, and many are proud of this, but we need strong controls to make it work. From a young boy I remember the problems of sectarianism in Northern Ireland and the conflict which it produced with thousands killed and injured. We have an uneasy peace, but the problem still exists and will probably erupt again.

The arrival in the 1960s and 1970s of large numbers from the West Indies caused resentment and tension as the British people were never consulted and there was racial tension on both sides. Enoch Powell made his emotive speech in parliament and was condemned for it, but he was supported by many people I met, and the British people's view was ignored. Shortly afterwards we joined the EU and lost control over the movement of people from Europe.

Having campaigned prior to the referendum I saw it was clear that stopping or reducing immigration was the main reason for voting to leave the EU. Immigration has not been controlled since even though about 75% feel it is too high. I am mystified as to why this is so because emerging problems are obvious. It is not that we should stop immigration totally but reduce the net figure to 100,000 a year or less so that people can be absorbed and integrated.

I was taught at school that Europe was the main centre for scientific, economic and military development over the last 500 years and that Britain was the leading and most powerful country. Certainly, Great Britain was at the forefront of scientific development and of the Industrial Revolution. We became the most powerful country in the world and created a massive empire.

The British empire was based on economic and military strength, but it would now seem that the days of empires are over and I believe unlikely ever to return.

My concern for the future is nothing to do with the decline of the British Empire. With few exceptions the countries Britain ruled are now independent, which I believe is best, with their own governments and sovereignty. It seems that empires do not last or perhaps cannot last due to the nature of human beings.

With what then am I really concerned? What are our deficiencies and problems? What is the cause of our problems? In what way are we declining? Is there any possibility of putting the problem right and if so, how? We may also ask if it really matters. Is there really a problem at all? This short book is a jumble of my thoughts and fears but my objective is to highlight the problems, make you think about it and hopefully you will join a political party to help solve our problems and make the right thing happen. It is astonishing that so few, particularly the young, join any political party, express their views and work to improve our society. Political parties should have millions of members, but they don't. We leave government to others then complain when we don't like the result.

Anyone who has no interest in politics has no interest in the future or concern for what is right and just. Think what matters to you and join a party, play a part in making things better and don't leave it to someone else. We are fortunate in Great Britain to have a democratic system which gives you an opportunity to play a part and influence the government. It is difficult because change is generally resisted and the powerful "establishment" who are doing well will do all in their power to keep things the way they are. Why do you think we have a House of Lords?

Don't let our country become like the communist world, like the dictatorships, those with military governments or worst of all those with religious regimes which take away freedom of choice. Governments often restrict people's rights and people forget they have duties too.

All Governments have ignored what I see as problems for the last 50 years, probably they think solving them would not get them elected. I think they are wrong, and the electorate are knowledgeable and care about the future but feel helpless and unheeded. To a very large extent the problems coincide with our joining the EU and losing control of our economy but may also be caused by other factors in this rapidly changing world.

I believe that if we take no action in the immediate future the situation will become progressively more difficult, and the future of this country and its people will suffer further decline and insecurity.

We need to ask ourselves a few questions and try to understand why things happen. If we do not ask questions, we won't understand why some systems are successful and others fail, we won't distinguish between truth and falsehood. We need to look at human nature and accept reality. It has been obvious for at least a century that the proliferation of humans and industrial development would lead to changes in the environment, but it has been ignored as no solution was evident and we always follow present needs because we are all selfish.

We can, of course, take no action and allow the natural world to adjust itself as it has always done. This is probably what will happen anyway. Alternatively, we can ask the questions, try and determine the world we would like to have and take the actions necessary, at least to try and put matters right., In a world with hundreds of countries, many different governmental systems and ideologies it will be difficult but hopefully not impossible to do.

What enabled the Egyptians and Romans to create Empires which lasted for many centuries. They were clearly economically sound, well organised and well governed. I understand however that they were societies beneficial to the rich and powerful but where most people lived in slavery or poverty. From what I have been taught the Roman Empire was described as a meritocracy. If you were strong and competent you gained respect and power if you were weak, low in intelligence or enterprise you lived in poverty. They had a system of government which supported power and continuity.

I get the impression that the British Empire was based almost entirely on trade and the creation of riches. Military power was used to protect and develop our trading activities. Inventiveness and enterprise were encouraged so that people in Britain were enabled to operate businesses efficiently to become rich and powerful. As Adam Smith said, "selfishness will always pay".

Very few people are inventive, very few can run successful businesses so in a free society some become powerful and wealthy, but most remain poor.

From the 16th century onward Europe appears to have made a great deal of economic and scientific progress. In Britain progress seemed to have moved ahead rapidly from the time of Elizabeth 1 but it may well have been triggered by Henry VIII taking over from the Catholic Church. This may be one of many factors, but I have no doubt that trading freedom and profit led to scientific discovery, investment in industry and commerce and the creation of wealth.

In Ireland, which remained Catholic, large numbers of the most intelligent, educated people went into the church becoming priests, monks or nuns, living off the working community and many families had too many children living in poverty. Many of the most enterprising of these emigrated and used their enterprise elsewhere. I'm sure that historians and other knowledgeable people will think differently and have better explanations for why some communities progressed and others did not. My personal experience of people however is that they are selfish and when self-interest is encouraged a society progresses.

Britain became one of the leading countries of the world at the forefront of scientific development and engineering so that our country became rich and powerful reaching its peak of power in the 19th century.

I regularly hear comments that Great Britain is a very rich country and certainly many of us live very good lives with reasonable housing, no shortage of food or clothing, our own transport, good holidays and endless entertainment. We have sick pay for those who cannot work, social housing, education to the age of 18 for our children and pensions for the elderly.

In the light of all this why should I, or anyone, have fears for the future? Certainly, none of our politicians appear to consider future problems, or if they do they don't talk about them or take any action. This short book is to invite you to think and decide if anything needs to be done. I believe we need to change our format of government and structure of society and pave the way for a better future rather than sit back and accept inevitable decline.

Britain's strength, wealth and prosperity came from commercial and industrial development. Productivity in the cotton and wool industries, due to newly invented machinery, increased by factors of 20 to 40 times. Britain also made massive progress, not only in spinning and weaving but in the production of chemicals, ceramics, steel and many other industries.

People of Europe, and Britain in particular was motivated to invent and run efficient, profitable businesses. Europeans became wealthy, perhaps the British most of all. Successful businesses reinvested their profit again and again.

By the year 1900 Great Britain had become one of the richest countries in the world, although there was an immense contrast between the wealthy landowners and industrialists and ordinary working people. I know from members of my family who were poorly educated working people, servants, labourers and craftsman that they had a poor standard of living, never owned a property and we're always under the controlling influence of the rich and powerful.

There is no doubt that changes began to take place at the beginning of the 20th century and were brought to a head by Britain's involvement in the First World War between 1914 and 1918.

I have tried to understand why Britain went into the First World War. On 28th June 1914 Archduke Franz Ferdinand and his wife were assassinated by a Serbian-backed terrorist after which European leaders made a series of political and military decisions. Austria-Hungary with German support declared war on Serbia on 28th July. Russia's support of Serbia brought France into the conflict. Germany declared war on Russia on 1st August and France on 3rd August. I am told Germany's violation of Belgian neutrality and fear of German domination of Europe brought Britain in on 4th August. Perhaps above all each country fearing that others could become too powerful. I believe Britain was afraid that if Germany overcame France and Belgium, it would become immensely powerful and a threat to British power and Empire.

I wonder what really the exact thinking of the governments of Britain, France, Russia and Germany was but fear, pride and intransigence made the war inevitable with all its horrific consequences. It was, of course, the ordinary working people who suffered most.

In each of the countries involved, propaganda encouraged patriotism, and vast numbers volunteered. On all sides millions were killed and injured, it was ordinary people who suffered the greatest losses, changing the attitude of working people towards their country's government. As a boy I remember the hatred my grandfather had, not for the Germans, against whom he had fought, but for the British commanders like Field Marshal Haig who directed the slaughter of so many of our soldiers. The suffering changed each country. Britain developed the Labour Party to represent ordinary working people.

I believe it was the final settlement between Germany and France in the punitive Treaty of Versailles, which created immense resentment in ordinary German people, which enabled the rise of fascism and the second even worse conflict. Many of you who read this will know the history better than I do and my understanding may be wrong, but I think the war of 1914-1918 undoubtedly brought about new thinking, changed or influenced the structure of social thinking. Working people took over the government of many countries, taking power away from the rich and aristocratic, and granted voting rights to the many if not all to choose governments. There was also the Russian Revolution in 1917 and the growth of communism.

The objective was to create a society with more equal rights for all, and to reduce deprivation and poverty. A fairer more equal society was the objective and to take power permanently away from a minority.

I wholeheartedly support these objectives. Fairness and equal opportunity for all seem morally correct. The question is how to achieve this, and whether socialist or communist thinking can be made to work well and achieve its intended objectives.

We certainly now have a declining economy and evolving social problems and my objective in this short book is to start people thinking of how our system needs to change if we are to have a safe and prosperous future.

CHAPTER 2

Britain's Major Current Problems.

THE FIRST ITEM to consider is the trading balance of payments considering both trade in goods and financial dealing.

I CANNOT RECALL EVER hearing a government minister express much concern about Britain's balance of payments or the "Current account balance" as I have heard it called.

The graph below shows our country's balance of payment for the last 50 years or thereabouts.

The recent figures are distorted because of the covid epidemic but the trend is essentially unchanged.

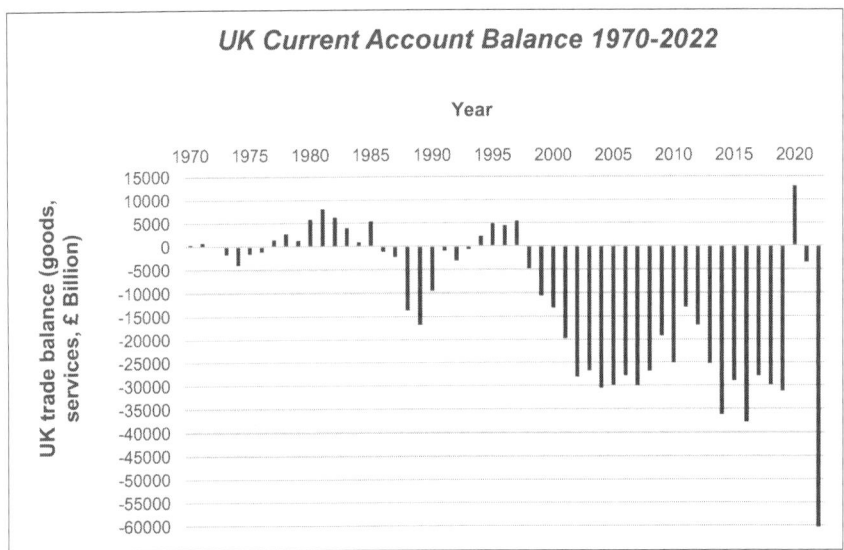

FIGURE 1: UK CURRENT ACCOUNT BALANCE 1970-2022 (OFFICE FOR NATIONAL STATISTICS, CENSUS 2021)

Prior to the mid-1970s international sales and purchases were approximately even. Since that time the gap has widened into what seems to be and ever-increasing deficit. In essence, as a country, we are spending vastly more than we are earning. In 2022, there was the astonishing deficit of £231 billion on trade in goods. This was offset by a surplus of £144 billion in services. This left our country with an overall trade deficit of

£87,000,000,000. Assuming the UK population is 65 million we effectively spent £1338 more than we earned for every member of the population.

I wonder why governments hardly ever talk about this situation. Perhaps they believe it isn't important. Maybe it isn't. However, it certainly gives me cause for concern because I always take a simplistic view.

Suppose for example for each member of your family, consisting of mum, dad and two children, you had overspent by £5,352 in 2022 (or £1338 each) and had been spending more than you had earned every year for most of the past 25 years. It is a shrewd guess that the debt collectors would be knocking on the door. As a family you would be in real trouble.

Suppose you were running a business and in 2022 you lost £1338 for each employee and had been making losses year after year. The business would soon go bankrupt and cease to exist.

My belief is that successive governments ignore the problem either because they don't know how to tackle it or know that the solution is extremely difficult and would be unpopular with the electorate. I personally think they prefer to ignore the problem and hope it will go away. It won't of course.

The business Great Britain UK Ltd. is in dire trouble and needs a new type of chief executive and board of directors with new ideas and methods. I suspect they will have to take a lot of unpleasant and unwelcome steps to rectify the situation.

How can the trading deficit situation have continued for so long? Where does the money come from to cover the deficit? My simple observations are that if you as an individual spend more than you earn, you have either to borrow the difference or sell some of your assets. If you don't you default on your payment and are in trouble.

Some of the deficit may be because we buy properties or businesses abroad, which is an investment. I don't know how I can find out the detail of this but I'm pretty sure that it is a small proportion of the total. We certainly buy much of our food from abroad, large amounts of oil, gas and other raw materials. We also buy quantities of clothing, household goods and other "stuff" from countries where labour is cheap and business operations are facilitated and often financially supported.

It is also evident, that buildings, land, and businesses are purchased by people and companies from abroad and large amounts of foreign money is borrowed. We all recall that our major football clubs are owned by people or companies from outside the UK. I now believe our postal service is being bought by a foreign owner who will run it as they wish and not necessarily as we would like.

What is the effect of having an adverse balance of payments. I'm sure all the expert economists will be able to correct me because, as I have said before, I am writing this as a layman, untrained and unqualified but interested in politics and experienced in business.

If you are having to borrow money there are inevitably costs so you are worse off. If you sell off your assets, you no longer have control of them. If you sell the majority of shares in a company, someone else controls that company, and will make decisions which are not necessarily in your interest. If you have no surplus money, you cannot purchase other businesses, properties or interests and are inevitably worse off.

I have often heard it said that Britain is one of the richest countries in the world, but we are losing ground rapidly. We are selling our assets, effectively living off our capital, a situation which needs to be corrected. I wonder what my readers think. Am I right in thinking that our trading deficit is a problem because I think it is most serious and very damaging to our country's future?

THE SECOND ITEM the national debt.

According to the taxpayers' alliance for the year 2021-22 the public sector net debt was £2,502.9 billion.

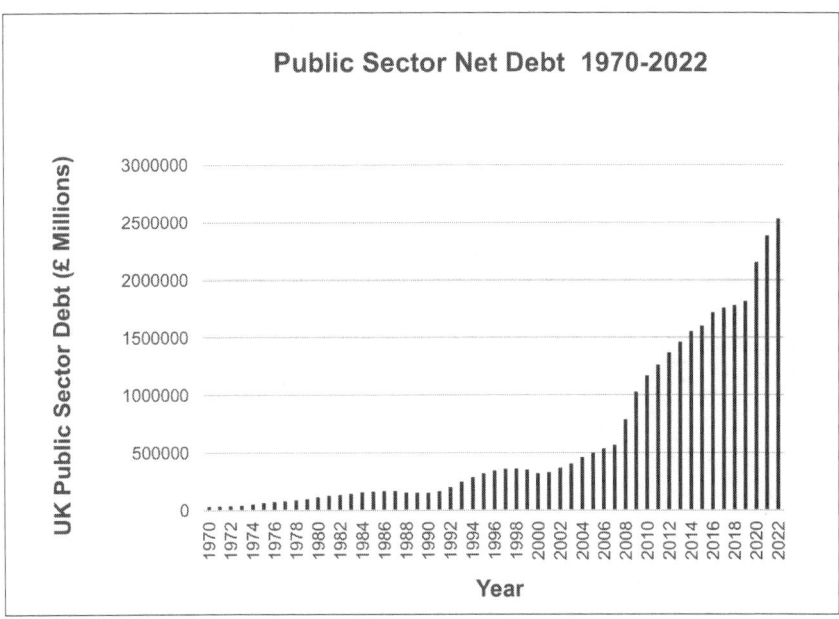

Figure 2: UK Public Sector Debt 1970-2022 (Office for Budget Responsibility)

Reducing the debt situation will be extremely difficult because we have a whole list of future commitments which include: -

State pensions for which I am quoted £5015 billion.

Public sector pensions I am quoted £1837 billion.

Private finance initiative £62 billion.

Nuclear decommissioning £159 billion

There is also an ongoing commitment to the National Health Service and many other public services as well as our defence and policing.

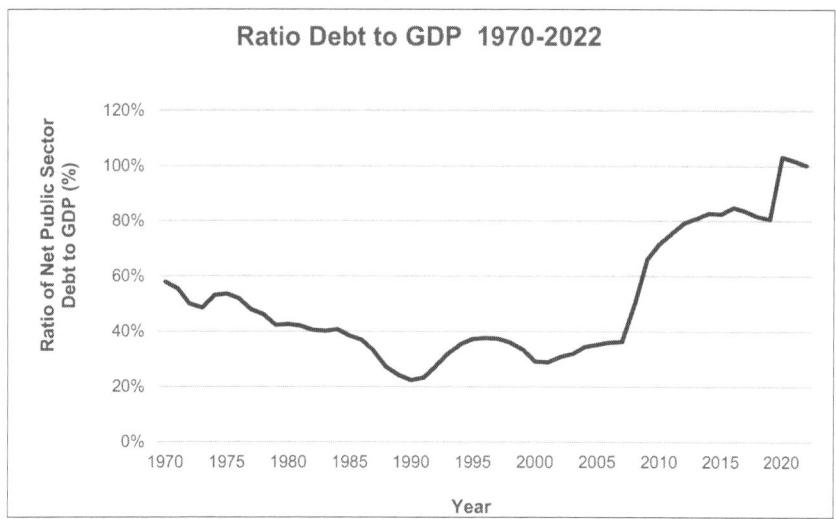

Figure 3: Ratio of Public Sector Net Debt to GDP (Office for Budget Responsibility)

This debt amounts to approximately £38,500 per person in the UK.

Interest payable on the public sector debt for 2023 is estimated at £112,000,000,000 or £1671 for every person in the UK assuming the population is about 67 million. I can't guarantee the accuracy, but it is based on government released figures. In simple terms for many, many years, government after government has seen fit to spend a great deal more money than it has received in taxation. Already the cost of borrowing is now the fifth biggest expenditure and in 10 years' time I am told it will be the third.

How can I describe what has happened, utter stupidity, madness, indifference or perhaps just total incompetence? Government after government has given in to the pressure of public want, spending vast amounts of money we don't have.

The effect of the national debt is that government budgets become more difficult because not only do they have to provide services for the present year, but they have to pay interest on the existing debt. They may of course also have to pay off some of the previous years' debts so the whole community is worse off.

The enormous national debt we have has come from excessive public expenditure which, having exceeded income, has led to the borrowing of significant money. We know that we need to pay for essential services such as the police and legal system, the defence of our country and services to support those who cannot care for themselves.

I must lay the blame for this at the door of socialist thinking which believes that we have to provide ever more and more public services by the state. I agree with the objectives but we have to find a different way of controlling our economy to achieve more equality and fairness and to take care of the sick and needy without more public spending, higher taxation or borrowing.

Personal Debt

I am given to understand the average personal debt in 2022 in the UK was £33,410 per adult. This I understand does not include household mortgage debt. There is also about £79 billion corporate debt which is money borrowed by companies to finance business.

Private debt is not the responsibility of government but is the responsibility of the individuals or companies who borrow and if they default the loss will be for the banks or other lenders and not the country as a whole.

It is not always a bad thing to borrow money. I have no regrets at borrowing money to purchase my first house, nor do I regret borrowing money to finance the development of my business or even obtaining a loan to purchase a car which enabled me to work more effectively. The problem of debt comes if it is excessive in relation to income.

There is a significant difference between borrowing money to invest and borrowing money to spend. How often have you heard government ministers say that they have invested "X" millions in-housing, education, transport etc, when in fact the money spent will never make a return.

HS2, Manchester Metrolink, and many other similar ventures are nice to have but a permanent burden on the taxpayer using up our resources and not adding to them. Would you invest your savings in such projects and hope to get it back with a profit? I certainly would not. Many leaders who run our government and our councils make decisions to undertake projects of this kind which are using other people's money without considering the long-term cost. These are some of the reasons why we have accumulated vast debts, which are ever increasing and very difficult to repay. Can we learn the lessons for the future?

Points to Consider

I certainly cannot guarantee that the figures quoted above are accurate. It is highly likely that they are not. Even government quoted official figures cannot be taken with any certainty purely due to human error and the difficulty of obtaining accurate information from innumerable sources.

They are certainly likely to be accurate to a small percentage which for our purposes in this thinking is good enough. The figures indicate a staggering adverse balance of trade and appalling ever increasing national debt.

I will discuss what I see as the primary causes, why I see them as being so dangerous and some suggestions as to what we should do. I hope those who read this will think about it and, if they think it matters, come up with their own solutions. We can of course, continue with our own self-interest, ignore the problem and do nothing about it and leave it to future generations. I'm all right Jack.

CHAPTER 3

Immigration and UK Population

THIS I BELIEVE is Britain's greatest problem because it is one that is difficult if not impossible to reverse. In 1974 the population of the United Kingdom was estimated at 56.23 million (already far too high). The official figure for 2023 was 67.736 million and is probably somewhat higher with a significant number of illegal immigrants uncounted. It has been estimated that by 2035 our population could be as high as 80 million.

The population of the Middle East, Africa, and central Asia is over 2 billion. In these areas there is mainly a poor standard of living, with many disputes and conflicts, and in many countries a severe lack of freedom and safety and millions will try to move to Europe and Britain.

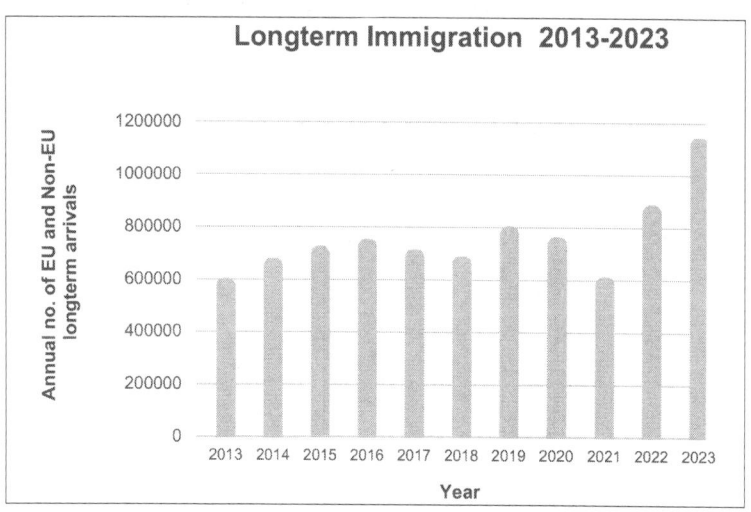

FIGURE 4: LONG-TERM IMMIGRATION INTO THE UK FROM EU AND NON-EU NATIONALS (OFFICE OF NATIONAL STATISTICS).

Britain is one of the most overpopulated countries in the world. We produce about half of our food and a quarter of our energy needs. We cannot afford to allow additional increases in our population.

Whether you are in favour of additional immigration or not it is imperative that our country has a system for controlling the immigration of people into Britain. Our membership of the EU meant we could not control our borders due to the policy of free movement of people and it is this which has caused the enormous increase in our population. The European Convention on Human Rights has made it almost impossible to remove immigrants, even those who came to Britain illegally or commit serious crime.

It is vital that we leave the European Convention of Human Rights so that we can control immigration to avoid possible problems in the future. Having left the European Union, why we have not done so beggars belief, but is largely because our members of parliament wanted to remain, as do large multinational companies. They want to ignore the referendum and the wishes of the British people.

Our streets are congested, towns polluted, schools overcrowded and there is a desperate shortage of housing despite building new houses at an enormous rate.

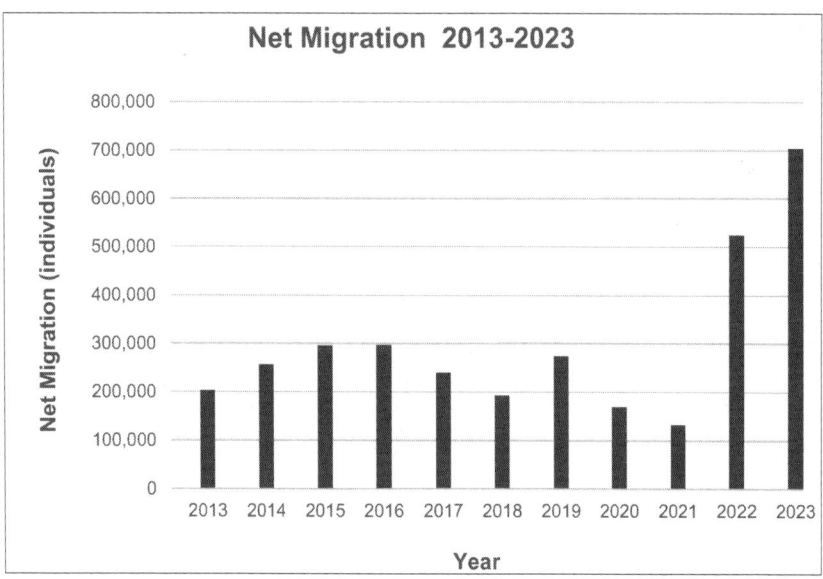

FIGURE 5: NET MIGRATION INTO THE UK (OFFICE OF NATIONAL STATISTICS)

The first action this government should take is to ask the people of Britain what policy on immigration they want, hold a referendum, and undertake that wish. The British Government makes the law, and it should reflect the wishes of the electorate, there can be no higher authority.

We have already been swamped and tens of millions more will come if we don't control it.

The present policy of the British government cannot work, and people will come in vast numbers costing billions of pounds because they know they can exploit our system.

What policy do we need? It must be decisive and very clear. What is the explanation for the present government allowing the current level of immigration when it is clearly against the wishes of the British people? The government want cheap labour which immigrants provide. They compete with our unskilled workers and keep wages down which inevitably creates poverty in the UK and thereby increases the need for welfare. The majority of immigrants send money back to their country of origin.

People wishing to arrive here should have to apply for a visa before starting out for this country. They must have a good reason for coming which should be to meet a British need and should have sufficient money to cover their stay. We should be issuing very few visas. The transport company, airline or shipping, should be responsible for ensuring that no one arrives without a visa and would have to return the passenger when it was not valid. There must be no right of application to court in these circumstances. There needs to be significant navy and army patrols in the channel and other parts of our coast and any illegal migrants should be returned immediately to the country from which they came and not allowed to land on the British coast. They could have applied to stay in the EU. If some did land they would be collected by the army held in a camps until returned. Under no circumstances should anybody who arrived illegally be allowed to stay and that policy needs to be made clear to everyone and rigidly enforced. Illegal arrivals would then stop.

I can understand that many people who believe in human rights will be outraged by this idea but if we don't act tens of millions will come and our country as we know it will be destroyed. The EU because of its policy of free movement, its human rights legislation and its proportional voting system will be unable to act. Civil disturbances will become highly likely.

A very small proportion of current immigration is from asylum seekers or illegal immigrants. The majority are given visas as students or workers followed by large numbers of their family members. Inevitably they then make every effort to stay and swell our already excessive population. The present government has caused this as though they wish to change our way of life with cheap labour and different cultures. It beggars' belief. Would it not be reasonable to ask the British people what they want and do that? Who could object apart from our members of parliament.? Are the government encouraging high immigration to deny the people's wishes as punishment for voting to leave the EU? Cheap immigrant labour is the main cause of our low wage high poverty economy. Many British people must live on low wages because immigrants, with whom they compete, will do so. Low labour costs suit many businesses which is why I believe the Government allows, indeed encourages high immigration. Never mind future problems. We need more efficient high wage businesses.

There are two distinct types of danger to our country caused by excessive immigration. At intervals through history there have been bad harvests. I understand these have been due to adverse weather conditions which have been attributed to volcanic action which polluted the atmosphere, reduced sunlight and temperature. The result was that millions starved. We are now faced with climate change or global warming which may well affect food production around the world. If we cannot import the food, we need people in Britain will go hungry. The higher our population the worse it will be.

From my experience and observation, a person's ethnicity has little to do with their abilities. It makes little difference as teachers, lawyers or doctors or as building workers, taxi drivers or even politicians. There are good and bad of every race. It does not alter the fact that racism exists and has a massive impact on people's lives. I have no doubt the killing of George Floyd would not have happened had he been white skinned, had he been white, there would have been no riots or protests once the perpetrator of his murder was prosecuted.

Far more important are cultural or religious differences. Antisemitism has existed for hundreds of years, not because Jewish people are bad but because they are different in belief and lifestyle, mixing and socialising in their own community to a large extent. In Britain we now have a large Muslim population I believe four or five million and growing rapidly. When my family owned an art gallery and restaurant there was a local Muslim population of 6-8000 within a mile or so but not one ever visited our premises. No doubt they assumed our meat was not halal, that we sold pork and alcohol of which they do not approve. Their reasons are understandable, even if founded on baseless beliefs, but the effect is divisive and a seedbed of hatred and violence.

America had its racial divide imposed upon it by slavery. Britain and Europe are creating their own racial and cultural divide by uncontrolled immigration with the naivety to assume problems will never happen or that we know how to handle it.

The people of Britain must decide whether these matters are problems and whether we need to take action or not. The readers of this little book must form their own opinion, decide whether any action is necessary, find a solution to our debts, control our borders and form a government which works for the people of Britain.

CHAPTER 4

Political Systems of Government

I AM NOT VERY qualified to write about this. I do however want to make my readers think about the subject for themselves.

It seems to me that in the early times military strength was the key, so that lesser groups were defeated and absorbed into the larger groups, and kingdoms formed which were ruled over by a single all-powerful monarch, the children of whom included the next king and formed the country's aristocracy. I get the impression it was a violent business with lots of fighting, the king often being replaced violently. It has also probably contributed to the dominance of men over women throughout history.

I have been told of the early democracies in Greece and Rome, but I get the impression that those appearing in the debating chamber of government, whoever they were, were almost certainly the leading most powerful families. Most poor working people and thousands of slaves having no choice whatsoever in government or legislation.

Several countries around the world had bloody revolutions getting rid of their kings to form republics. I may be wrong, but I believe violence was used in the majority if not on every occasion. It is only in recent years that any system of voting has been used to bring about changes in government.

As far as I can determine all communist governments took over by force, as did most of the fascist governments and once in power prevented any further free elections. The re-election of Putin in Russia seems a questionably fair election and opposing him a risky business.

The most important feature of governments is that they were strong, had authority, and the ability to enforce their own laws particularly over their own people. It is still important they are strong today and have the power to govern but a non-violent system for change is even more important.

In Britain a parliament gradually emerged but those in it, and who voted for it, we're aristocratic or wealthy. The power of the monarch has been reduced to almost nothing, the House of Lords had its power limited, power now being vested in the elected House of Commons, but it leads me to think of what we need to change now.

During my working life when I ran a series of small businesses it became obvious that my staff and customers did not like change. It was necessary, for my business to be profitable, to update both my equipment and procedures. The change from manual typewriters to electronic and from electronic typewriters to computers was severely resisted but eventually welcomed when the benefits became evident. For many years I ran an agency for the Halifax bank. When an ATM was installed in our office people initially came to the counter to withdraw money, particularly the older customers. My staff showed them how to use the cash machine and eventually it's use was adopted and became preferred.

In politics change is even more difficult because it involves the need for some to relinquish power and the wealth and privilege which goes with it. In Britain we had to fight to get the vote for men and then for women and all the welfare benefits. Many countries got rid of their monarchies, all I think by revolution. Racist regimes in Rhodesia and South Africa had to be overthrown and despite the Bill of Rights

America is still racist. Communist and fascist regimes strenuously hold on to power often imprisoning people who seek change. Religious regimes, particularly Christian and Muslim, still hold on to power and dictate a way of life to their communities.

I'm proposing changes to our system. Changes which I believe will make our system fairer, improving equality and diminish privilege.

I'm certain that any change will be severely resisted because those presently in power in Britain will hold onto their power and privilege with every ounce of strength they have as governments and religious authorities have always done in the past.

CHAPTER 5

The Present Government Structure

IN BRITAIN THERE were a series of civil wars leading to the defeat of the Royalists and the execution of the King, Charles 1. Oliver Cromwell was then appointed Lord Protector and Britain was effectively a republic from 1649 to 1660. By 1660 Oliver Cromwell himself had died and he had appointed his son Robert as his successor but there was no satisfactory system for choosing a successor so in 1660 the monarchy was restored and Charles 11 crowned King.

The Republic failed because it did not have a successful means of ensuring sound continuity.

Britain retained its monarchy together with a parliament. It was made up of the rich and aristocratic with only the wealthy males allowed to vote.

Gradually it has evolved to the present state with a "Constitutional Monarch" with little power, the House of Lords, partly inherited and partly appointed, and a House of Commons all elected on a one vote per person system which provides the government of today.

Head of State

In a system of fairness and equality, we should clearly have the most preferred person chosen as head of State. Anyone could stand for Head of State with everyone voting and the one attracting the most votes would be appointed. The head should be re-elected at suitable intervals. Surely this would be the fairest structure.

The head should be re-elected every parliament or whatever period is workable. This is surely the right structure as they are representatives of the British people.

The "Head of State" position without any power would be unappealing and would be unlikely to attract quality applicants (this may not be important) if they get no authority as a result. The alternative is to emulate the presidential system of the United States.

The American system of electing a president who is very powerful, has in my view produced a few excellent presidents and a fair number of very poor ones. The present situation in the United States gives the people a choice between two old men, neither of whom in my view, is suitable to lead the world's most powerful economy. If the president was elected by and from the Senate and House of Representatives there would probably be a sounder president and less conflict between the President and the elected houses. This is just a thought but the responsibility of the American people.

Queen Elizabeth 11 was a good Head of State, devoted her life to the role and handled it well. It never seems proper to me however, that one group of human beings should be considered "Royal" or "Their Majesties" and that the titles of "Princes", "Dukes" and "Lords" are used. It is the very essence of a state of inequality and privilege which fairness cannot justify.

It is quite evident however that a very large number of the British people enjoy and admire our Royal family. I remember the immense crowds at the coronation, royal weddings and funerals. We all recall the astonishing show of affection, and tears of love and sadness when Princess Diana died. For reasons I personally find incomprehensible most people appear to want to pay deference to those they perceive as "Royal", "Aristocratic" or "Upper class."

This characteristic does not seem to be restricted to Britain, Our Royal family are astonishingly admired throughout the world and although I would personally change the situation it is one, we must retain as our monarchy is supported by popular opinion.

Several years ago I asked members of my family and other people I knew, what impact the Royal family had on their lives. Without exception the answer was none, and few had ever attended a Royal Event.

The cost of the Royal family is about £1.30 per year per person which seems small. It is about £85 million a year plus significant amounts on the maintenance of palaces.

I am told however that the Royal family attract a lot of trade, though this seems to be more supposition than fact. We clearly must retain our Royal head of state because the public enjoy and admire them but if you think about it carefully the concept is wrong and helps to maintain privilege and inequality.

If it was ever to be changed, I would have our Head of State from and chosen by our elected government as a constitutional head without power.

House of Commons

We all know it is from amongst the members of this House that the government is formed, and it is here that the power lies to govern the country, to make and amend our laws, set taxes and agree expenditure.

There are normally 650 members of the House of Commons each representing a fixed area of land we call a constituency. I understand the number is about to be reduced to about 600. The elected member is the person attaining the largest number of votes in the constituency and once elected is deemed to represent the people of that area but clearly doesn't. It is common for the elected person to have obtained less than 50% of the vote, sometimes as little as a third or less of the votes cast.

Most people standing for election represent one of the political parties. Labour, Liberal. Conservative, Scottish Nationalist, Plaid Cymru, Green Party, etc. Only in exceptional circumstances can anyone get elected who does not represent one of the main parties.

The governing party must have a majority in the House of Commons in order to get its legislation passed and if no party has an overall majority one of the largest parties may govern with the help of one or more of the smaller parties but may be restricted in what it can do.

Each party publishes a manifesto or statement of its policies so that voters can choose which party to vote for, but I am told very few people read the manifestos.

It sounds like a very good system until you look carefully at how it works. First, each party chooses its own leader so at the election. Conservatives, Labour, Liberal etc will have a chosen leader and the leader of the party with most seats will become Prime Minister. Generally, the party leadership, together with advisors set the policies in their manifesto and the campaign to get members elected will almost certainly concentrate on a few policies the party thinks will be popular and get it elected. At the last election Boris Johnson, the leader of the Conservative Party promised to "Get Brexit Done" which dominated all other policies in the election campaign and won his party the election.

Having been elected with a majority of Conservative supporters Mr Johnson then formed the government and decided which legislation to pursue in the coming parliamentary session. If you had been elected as a conservative member of Parliament, you would be expected to vote with the party even on policies you didn't agree with. You would be likely to be thrown out of the party if you didn't do so. The power of deciding what to do rests almost entirely with the Prime Minister who is supported by a cabinet of some 30 members who are unlikely to oppose the PM significantly, as they would lose their job in the cabinet and possibly as a member of Parliament. When it comes to a vote in the House as a whole, the party issues a "three-line whip" compelling all members of the party to support the party line. Individual members of a party have no say and no power other than to support their party against the opposition to get legislation passed. If about 600 of the members of Parliament were not present it would make virtually no difference to the legislation passed into law.

I'm not quite sure how we come to have 650 members of Parliament, now reducing to 600, As most MPs have no power there seem to me to be far too many. Those who are in the House of Commons would have no wish to reduce the numbers as they would lose their seats, incomes and privilege. It is therefore difficult to change the House of Commons. I am pleased that a reduction of 50 is now taking place.

During my time as a supporter of one of the political parties (and I have been a member of the Labour Party, Liberals, Conservatives and UKIP), I never heard anybody suggest we should change the content or structure of the House of Commons. Most people think it is satisfactory and I believe they think that way because sometimes their party attains power and, in any event, they do have a vote and probably never give a thought to what might be wrong. Let me think of some of the features we might change.

First. Why do we need 650 members or even 600, when they can't even all have a seat in the debating chamber?

Second. The elected member in a constituency is there to represent all constituents. Voters would not want to write to an MP who was not from the party they supported.

Third. Many MPs have other jobs earning large amounts of money instead of tackling the problems of the country for which they were elected.

Fourth. Who do you vote for if there are policies in each manifesto which you don't like?

Fifth. What do you do and whom do you vote for if none of the candidates has a policy which you really wish to support? For example, if you are opposed to HS2, want to limit immigration, and of course wanted to leave the European Union.

Sixth. Many people vote for a party, not because they support it, but because they are opposed to another party they really dislike. They vote to get the party they dislike out.

Seventh. Is the method of choosing the candidates for a constituency satisfactory? About 50 years ago I was present at a union meeting with my father-in-law where all members of his Union had been instructed to vote for a particular candidate who would stand for the Labour Party. I, of course, not being a union member could not vote but the vote was unanimous even though my Father-in-Law and those who were with him didn't know anything about the candidate. I remember years later when I was at a conservative meeting to select the parliamentary candidate. Nine members of the party had applied to stand for selection but seven of them were eliminated at a closed meeting between three members of the committee and a group at conservative head office. The reasons for the elimination were not given, and the committee members were sworn to secrecy. This kind of practice, which I think you will find is common means, that candidate selection is underhand, one might say devious and is corrupt. Why would you want to keep the reasons secret if the decisions were fair?

The establishment is hard at work to make sure the system doesn't change. So how might we change the House of Commons?

I would ask my readers to think for themselves and decide what they would like the function of the House of Commons to be and how it should be structured and work.

I know most members of Parliament have no power and little influence on national government policy and in the main cannot have any impact on the legislation of the Parliament. The Prime Minister and the Cabinet, selected by him, have all the power, decide what legislation will be undertaken. The remaining members of Parliament have little influence on policy or decision-making.

When it comes to voting on government policy members of Parliament, who are not in the cabinet, are forced to vote to support the government policy and the opposition are generally forced to vote against it. It would make no difference if there were 100, 200 or even 400 fewer members. The voting results would be the same approving the legislation of the party in power.

Of course, members do have some influence and regularly agitate to achieve minor projects requested by their constituents.

Members of Parliament often pride themselves in undertaking " constituency work" and hold regular "surgeries" meeting members of their constituency who have requests or problems. I suggest you give this some thought and see if you agree with me. I would dispense with the idea of constituency involvement for members of Parliament. I would ensure that if people have a request for support or action, they contact the party of their choosing.

Most people contacting their MP are in what I call the "I want, we want, someone needs" category. They want their MP to get them, a better house, more allowance, road speed change, other local want. My view is that this is not what members of Parliament should be doing. I'm repeating myself again because it is just wrong. Surely the needs of the community should come first.

I would reduce the number of members of Parliament drastically. I think about 200 to 300 would be sufficient and all members of the governing party would have a function in national government which is what Parliament should consider its main obligation.

Under the present system members of Parliament are assessed locally by constituents interested in local issues and supported at the next election. In other cases, voters chose a party to vote for and give no thought for the local candidate. My father used to say that in his constituency you could put up a pig with a blue ribbon as the candidate and it would get in.

This creates what has regularly been described as the Postcode Lottery whereby some constituencies have better services than others because either their member of Parliament is aggressively active or perhaps from the governing party rather than the opposition.

Most needs are not local, the education of a 10-year-old girl in Brighton is no different from Chester, the care and support of an elderly man, the need for jobs or healthcare are the same throughout the country. Most local influence leads to inequality and unfairness and should not influence members of Parliament.

It also regularly means that desperate national requirements are not fulfilled because of local opposition instead of undertaking actions in the total national interest. NIMBY is alive and well.

Surely the national interests of all people in the country and its overall economic well-being must take precedence over local wishes.

I cannot however imagine parliament allowing any such changes.

House of Lords

It is questionable whether a second chamber or house is necessary. What is probably sensible is for proposed legislation by any government to be debated and reviewed but you cannot have the seat of power in two places, or nothing will get done and there will be constant conflict between the two authorities. Conflict has regularly existed between the House of Commons with its elected members and the House of Lords.

For the second chamber to exist at all it must be just a "Review Chamber" but it has not been structured in the past in that form. The unelected House of Lords can still reject legislation or delay it, a situation which is totally unacceptable.

There has often been talk in the past of reforming the House of Lords, but nothing done has been fundamental. The Conservative / Liberal Coalition attempted a review which was cancelled in 2012. Prior to that the Labour government had reformed the House of Lords in an act originally started in 1997 which was adopted in 1999 whereby the number of hereditary peers was reduced to 92 the remainder being appointed plus bishops from the Church of England. In my view it was worse than the original House of Lords and the appointment process, as always, fosters favouritism and privilege. The House of Lords as it now stands is undemocratic and completely unacceptable.

Apart from the 92 hereditary peers we now have almost 800 appointed members of the House of Lords many of these are ex-members of Parliament, people who have supported the parliamentary parties and those who reap the reward for services to the establishment.

It is the greatest club of privilege in the world, immensely expensive and undermines our true democracy.

This house needs to be replaced by an elected chamber whose main function is to re-examine proposed legislation to ensure it meets the requirements of the British public.

Throughout my lifetime there has been discussion about reform but a great reluctance to change anything. This is not surprising as it is a wonderful place to end your political career amongst a group of self-interested people working as a body to maintain the status quo. It is the centrepiece of the establishment, anti-democratic and anti-change, supporting the rich and powerful at the expense of ordinary people.

Reform of the House of Lords should be the first item of change by the next Labour government. Removing hereditary peers, replacing appointed life peers and Bishops of the Church of England by an elected chamber. We certainly cannot continue, if we are to remain a respected democracy, with an unelected house. My basic suggestions are as follows,

1) It should be called the Review Chamber or Review House.
2) It should have about 100 members possibly as many as 200.
3) Its functions should be to examine proposed legislation by the government, assess the implications and effects that legislation will have and recommend to the government appropriate amendments.
4) The members should be elected on a proportional representation basis. The members of each party should select the members of their party who can stand. Any member should be able to put themselves forward to stand, and they should get seats in the chamber based on the number of votes.
5) The election should take place at the same time and for the same period as normal parliamentary elections.
6) The House should handle referenda (see later suggestion).
7) The House should provide the chairperson for public, or government enquiries and they should be appointed by the Review House not by the government.

8) Members of this Review Chamber should serve in the cabinet. Probably 5 or 6 but not for a specific ministry.

Note: An alternative method of electing this house could be to elect members by profession. One seat could exist for farmers and farm workers, one for the medical profession one for engineers etc. The electorate would have to nominate their category when they registered to vote and if they did not register a particular category their vote would be for a Party member on a proportional representation basis.

My suggestion would be that the House of Lords is immediately abolished. And the House of commons given one year to establish details of a replacement house managing without a second house for that period.

I cannot think of any good reason for retaining the House of Lords. It is fundamentally undemocratic, it fosters discrimination and privilege, there is no fair and just way of appointing members, it is ridiculously costly and to include Bishops of the Church of England is staggeringly unjustifiable.

There will be many suggestions other than mine so think them out and let us get something done.

CHAPTER 6

Local Government

PEOPLE ARE RATHER proud of having local government. Local government is in many forms, metropolitan borough council's, county councils, town councils even parish councils. The idea is that local people can try and influence what happens in their own area allegedly to meet the needs of the local community. In recent years many major cities have elected mayors who are a powerful voice to get what is wanted by their local community. We have devolved parliaments for Scotland, Wales and Northern Ireland.

In the same way that central government has grown step-by-step over the centuries so has local government.

I get the impression that local government is popular because in any given area there is a body of authority working for the local community. They are there to organise public services, local transport, education, housing, social services, parks and open spaces, planning, environmental health services and many more activities. There is somebody to talk to about local problems and somebody who may help those who require support.

The whole idea sounds good to me that there is somebody I can choose to represent me on local issues. It is good occasionally, to do what hardly anyone ever does and ask yourself a few questions about how it works, who pays, is everything always above board, is expenditure sensibly controlled, and are the objectives sensible?

Running a local authority is big, big business often involving hundreds of millions even billions of pounds of expenditure. The first question we should ask is whether the elected councillors and those who are employed by the council are competent to handle such sums of money in a wise and efficient way. My personal experience is that this is almost never the case. This may seem to be a criticism of democratically elected people, but I say it because having run businesses myself there are hundreds of actions by the local authority that as a businessman I most definitely would not do, and public money is put at risk for political objectives.

Consider a parish council in a small village. A few people are elected as councillors and local people will approach them with their problems. Several people may ask for a bus service to the nearest town. The councillors will consider this and try to get it done to please the people and get elected next time but if the bus route doesn't pay the cost will eventually be added on the local council tax. Members of the public may ask for street lighting, traffic calming measures and many other issues. Councillors will inevitably try to meet this need to maintain their popularity. Hardly ever do they ask the members of the public if they are happy for additional expenditure. In public affairs public services come before costs even when they are little used and could be available from private sources.

The same problem applies throughout all local government and because of publicity and the desire to be re-elected public expenditure increases and increases providing ever more in-depth services at the expense of the taxpayer.

It is questionable whether in local governments either the councillors or the council employees have the expertise to undertake major projects.

When we hear of people being homeless, sick. or short of food it is impossible not to want to help them. Old people need care and support, The single mum with three small children needs a home and income, we cannot leave orphaned children unaided. The difficulty is in deciding where not to help.

Should expenditure levels take priority or public services? Would it be reasonable to ask the electorate each year whether they would like the council tax for example, to be increased by 2%, remain the same as the previous year, or decreased by 2%. the council employees would then have to provide services in accordance with the money available. Now the councillors and council employees decide what they would like to do and simply charge the householders the amount it costs. Worse still they often borrow money for a project which is nice but not essential and leave the community with large ongoing debt.

The ever-increasing cost of public services is the cause of our financial difficulties. The public now always ask local authorities and the government for more and more. Better housing, cheaper transport, more money for this and that and the Taxpayer is expected to pay. Recently I have heard demands for compensation for those affected by electricity pylons, support for drug addict rehabilitation, help for families with a child with behavioural or other mental problem. There is some additional demand every day all of which are difficult to refuse but all add to the problem.

Let us for a moment consider a transport system. This can be provided by the local authority and some routes would be purely to provide a public service even where the number of users is far below an economic level. Sometimes it is thought necessary to provide free travel for elderly people, the disabled and unemployed. Those people apply to the local authority for a bus pass which is a costly process. They then must provide a system to compensate service providers the fee for carrying the people who don't pay. Additionally, of course those receiving free travel will make some unnecessary journeys simply because it costs them nothing. Services of this type, cost enormous amounts of money and make the whole community poorer, nice as the services seem to be.

A privately run transport system will tailor itself to the need eliminating services which are not used or too little used. Perhaps with local authorities the activities should be restricted to those tasks which cannot be done by private enterprise. Every reader should think about this carefully. The cost of our debt is a major item which prevents more cost-effective spending.

It is always difficult to get exact information about public services, but I believe the following information is a reasonably accurate assessment of local government in the UK.

I understand that in total there are 343 local authorities.

County councils, district council's, unitary authorities, metropolitan borough councils, London boroughs.

Between them they employ approximately 1 million people and provide 800 different services.

There are about 8800 elected councillors and I understand that they are each paid £8744 (2023) for their services though some are paid additional amounts for further responsibilities.

This comes to a total of approximately 76 million pounds.

In total for the year 2020/21 I am informed local authorities spent £114,722,000,000. If we assume the population is 65 million it is £1765 for every person or there abouts.

Having worked in business for over 50 years, about 10 years, as an employee of a large company and for 40 years running my own small businesses, I realise that there is very different thinking and objectives in running businesses for profit from running a local authority or government department where the objective is to provide a service.

In a commercial enterprise the owner or manager will have as his objective the making of profit or at least income. They will try to make the business as efficient as possible always trying to reduce costs and provide as good a service as possible to attract more trade. If the operation fails to make a profit and is not cost-effective it will soon be closed and cease to exist, but it will not be a cost to the public.

If I am running a taxi service, I need to attract customers but at the same time I must charge a fee which will cover the cost of labour, fuel, etc. There can be no income that is not paid by the customer.

A public transport system provided by the local authority, or national operator may run services which are not economic, are not paid for in full by the users but are supported from taxation. Many of our rail services, bus and tram services are highly subsidised.

This does not mean they are not worthwhile and very valuable, but it is easy for them to become ever more costly, a burden on the taxpayer, spending money which would be far better spent in other ways.

As a manager of a public body such as, environmental health, public transport, social services, refuse collection, etc. we are far more likely to be judged by the service we give rather than the cost. If we provide a service to the public, we are more likely to ignore efficiency than in a private business as we can increase taxes to cover extra costs. Private businesses constantly try to increase their prices but are restrained by competition and therefor are constantly mindful to become more efficient.

I have observed local authorities over my 40 years in private business, they have only paid attention to costs when forced to do so, they have regularly provided costly unnecessary services and followed agendas which are unjustified and frequently inexplicable.

I learnt in business that the most important tasks are the ones you can avoid doing altogether. In local authorities there are many of these which no one considers, where public services are not self-funding it generally means there is insufficient demand.

In essence local authorities should not undertake any tasks themselves but allocate them to private businesses who will have to make themselves cost effective.

I would establish an investigative body made up of accountants, and experienced entrepreneurs to look at all public services with a view to cutting costs where possible. This would enable a significant reduction in taxation and provide funds to be spent more effectively elsewhere.

Most politicians, in both parliament and local authorities are primarily concerned with the provision of public services. They are constantly bombarded by the public to provide or improve some service or other. It may be public transport, refuse collection, better social housing, a new swimming baths or other sport facilities. The demand, some would call it need, is constantly increasing. The beneficiary is often paying little or nothing directly towards the cost and perceives the services as free, whereas in fact they are paid for indirectly by the taxpayer. There is therefor pressure on all candidates for Local Authorities and Parliament to provide more, and better public services to satisfy the electorate. To meet the cost money must be raised by taxation, which is now at one of the highest rates ever, or by borrowing money which adds to future costs.

We need to reduce public spending drastically and wherever possible remove public services from local authorities. We need to have a Parliament which legislates in the national interest, not the local one, and stop parliamentarians undertaking constituency work which pressures them to spend more money to get elected.

Perhaps you can think of other solutions or are happy to see our country have ever increasing debt and decline.

The Civil Service

It is responsible for administering government policy, delivering public services, and collecting taxes. It is politically neutral supporting the government of the day and providing continuity. No government can manage without the Civil Service.

As a member of the public, I'm surprised how little I know about the Civil Service.

Around about 500,000 people are employees in the Service many of whom are to do with tax collection and the payment of pensions and benefits.

I'm assured the Civil Service makes every attempt to recruit competent people so that they can give to the government the best possible support services to enable the implementation of the policies of the government of the time.

I'm also assured that they recruit people who have been successful in business to ensure that the Civil Service is efficient and capable.

I am none the less astonished at the number of people employed in the Service as it is entirely tax funded and according to Wikipedia the civil service pays an additional 27% of employees' salaries into employee pensions whereas in private business the employer pays in about a quarter of that or less. I am informed that all employer contributions are to be increased in line with the constant desire for more and more welfare, but I question if this is the right policy. Outside the state pension most of the funding of pensions should be by the employee.

The Civil Service like local authorities is a great concern to me because of the costs involved. I would ask you as a voter to think about this and decide what should be done.

According to my internet research public spending in the year 2019/20 was £842 billion.

Public sector income in the year 2021/22 was £862 billion or £31,000 per household. 37% of GDP or thereabouts.

This income is of course taxation and should be reduced significantly. The question is how this can be done and still enabled essential public services to operate satisfactorily.

I find it difficult to obtain any recent published costs for the Civil Service but there are about 500,000 employees at an average cost of £40,000 each which is about 20 billion pounds or £300 per member of the population. There are, of course, all the additional operating costs.

I would set a target of reducing the costs of the Civil Service by about 50%. This will take many years and can only be done by simplifying the taxation system, pensions and other legislation. Eliminate any services which are choice rather than necessity. It will be hated by many but must be done to avoid more debt and inevitable disaster.

My readers must think whether we can allow ever increasing debt. Do you have any other solution? We must either cut public spending or increase our income.

CHAPTER 7

Referenda

I HAVE OFTEN HEARD members of Parliament; members of the press and others speak with disdain when a politician panders to popular opinion. They refer to it as populism which they despise and regard populists contemptuously even though a populist is a person who seeks to appeal to the interests and wishes of ordinary people. This may initially seem the opposite of what I am recommending.

The opposite is generally true of governments and members of parliament who think they know best and was particularly evident to me in the European Union where every effort was made to preserve the union as it was conceived by the leadership without considering the wishes of the people.

Surely a true democracy should basically be to run the country to increase the wealth of the nation providing safety and security for most.

The referendum held about our membership of the European Union in which a slight majority voted to leave was a very good example of the need for referenda.

A system therefore needs to be introduced whereby a referendum can be held on issues which governments may not choose as their important items of legislation.

The EU referendum was a good example, as without it the views of the people would not have been assessed, as all political parties were in favour of remaining and not representative of the popular view. I wonder what would happen if other European Union countries were allowed a choice?

Holding referenda is extremely difficult because it must be a simple decision, yes or no, leave or remain, do it or cancel it. It can therefore only be used for basic issues.

Examples could be, build or don't build HS2, introduce capital punishment, stop illegal immigration.

To have a referendum a petition would probably have to be held, I would suggest controlled by the Review Chamber and when enough signatures have been obtained, research would be undertaken, and the appropriate decision put to the electorate.

Holding two or three in each four-year parliamentary period could do nothing but good for our democracy. Ordinary people are important and much more understanding than most parliamentarians believe.

CHAPTER 8

Taxation

OCCASIONALLY I SPEAK to academics, senior teachers and professional people who are happy to pay their tax for the benefit of society. They seem in the main to be quite well-off people, with decent incomes and can easily afford to pay more. They mostly have enjoyable jobs which are rewarding in themselves and are generally supporters of the Labour or Liberal parties, perhaps the Greens. I have never met a self-employed person who thinks that way, perhaps there are some.

Tax has been hated through the centuries to the extent that people built up their windows to avoid the window tax.

The impact of taxation is something I have talked about often, here I go repeating myself again.

Not only do most people dislike paying tax or feel they pay too much but taxation makes them take actions they otherwise would not do.

Some entrepreneurs do take action to avoid making payment both legally and fraudulently but more important they make little decisions which are bad for the economy. If they feel the government taxes them too much or that taxes may increase further, they may lose confidence and cancel or delay the development of their business. Having paid significant amounts of tax it may leave an investor short of capital for business development which they would have to borrow. Some may decide this is risky and not proceed with business development. The lower taxes are the more likely it is for a businessperson to expand

and increase business activity. High taxes drive investors abroad, lower income, reduce investment, and increase imports.

For centuries working people lived in poverty. They were exploited by the wealthy aristocracy in mining, farming and the cotton and wool industries, not least by the religious elite who lived to a high standard at the expense of the poor. It is not surprising that the Labour party was created to give working people a share in power and to make laws for the protection of all. Although there is still some exploitation there are now opportunities for all who work to take them.

Some "Left Wing" members of the Labour Party have a hatred of the wealthy and want to penalise the rich. The right policy is to support the inventor and the entrepreneur to create wealth and better jobs for working people. "Don't kill the goose that lays the golden eggs"

CHAPTER 9

About People.

Equality, Giving Everyone a Fair Chance

THE BASIC OBJECTIVES of the Labour Party to support and represent ordinary working people, to ensure equal rights in all circumstances, and to reduce and if possible, eliminate poverty is an objective we should all wholeheartedly support. We should always give our support to the disadvantaged, to those who are sick, whether mentally or physically, to those whose lives are blighted by being born into a poor environment or into a neglectful or damaged family and those who through circumstances outside their control end up disadvantaged. The doors of opportunity, for education, rehabilitation and retraining should always be open creating ways to a better life for all,

The Labour Party's solution to these problems has in many ways led to significant improvements in employment rights, pensions, sick pay, universal education and health services, all of which are welcome. Had it not been for the Labour Party much of this would not have happened particularly as the wealthy and aristocratic perceived ordinary working people as a lower form of humanity which could never aspire to their own standards.

To fund much of what has happened in the past to improve working lives higher taxes were introduced. It was an attempt to redistribute wealth. Inheritance tax, income tax and many others were levied to fund these benefits and many additional public services. Forgive me for repeating myself yet again.

The question now is where do we go from here? We have got to the stage where increasing taxes does not increase revenue, deters effort and increases unemployment.

In communist countries where collective ownership was established productivity declined, people became poorer and often starvation followed. It was made worse when energetic enterprising people were penalised and as a result poverty increased. Many socialists see entrepreneurs as greedy selfish people and want to take from them their businesses and wealth with the result that business declines and national wealth reduces.

Labour party members also wish to introduce greater public ownership, state-run industries and public services which lack the entrepreneur's motivation for efficiency and economy leading to greater costs, significant waste, poorer productivity and less wealth.

To solve the problems of poverty we need to increase the wealth of the nation. This can only be done by encouraging enterprise, improving efficiency of business, ensuring the availability of investment and promoting work. Work needs to be readily available, education encouraged with training and retraining to meet the changing world. Motivation must be greatly in favour of working as opposed to unemployment and benefit subsistence. Perhaps most of all taxation must be drastically reduced and self-sufficiency encouraged.

Most labour supporters will be unhappy at the idea of reducing taxation, of limiting benefits, eliminating public ownership or reducing it to a minimum and privatizing public services. In many ways, our society has taken away personal responsibility, and this must be restored. We should all be responsible for looking after ourselves and our families and I propose a system which enables people to do that by their own endeavour. This does not mean of course that we neglect to care for those who are sick or incapable of caring for themselves.

I have mentioned on several occasions the need to reduce taxation. My reasons for this are simply because it is evident from all our actions that we don't like paying tax. Every accountant advises businesses about how to reduce their tax payment, people regularly want to work for cash to avoid tax, smuggling is rife and undertaken by many who go abroad and can get something tax free, and we've all heard of people who don't want to work overtime because the effort is too great for the reward because of tax. Businesses trading in cash don't always report all their takings.

I told you before, I worked for a foreign company for some years and although never openly stated, the policy was not to pay UK taxes and goods were imported into Britain at vastly inflated prices to avoid UK Tax by exporting the profit.

Every day individual people make decisions about business. Is it worth expanding they ask themselves? I will have to borrow money to do so because my previous profit was taken in tax and borrowing puts me at risk. Some will decide not to expand, others will decide not to invest at all so jobs will not be created. The more we encourage the entrepreneur and the inventor the more and better jobs we create to the benefit of all.

We must not discourage enterprise but harness it, encouraging as many people as possible to become wealthy, to create efficient industry and better paid jobs. In the following section I proposed to illustrate how we can encourage business, create greater wealth, improve our environment and better standards for everyone. It must however include systems which protect the rights and opportunities of all.

I would like you to join me in thinking about some of the most important aspects of all our lives. Housing, health care, transport and food supply are important to us all. I want to think how some things could be done differently both to improve how systems perform and reduce the costs as the best way to reduce taxation is to make our systems and services efficient and reduce expenditure.

Services for public use are important, indeed essential. These include the establishment of roads and railways, the provision of public transport, pensions and welfare, medical services and care for those in need.

There are however questions we need to ask about these. Is it necessary for them to be provided by state or local authority services? Are all the services necessary at all? Can they be done in a cheaper more efficient way? What happens when we provide services free of charge or subsidised from taxation? It appears to be a natural policy of Labour Party supporters to provide more and more services through the public sector, to consider provision of services as paramount, the costs less important.

When I have examined the services of local authorities and government departments they have, without exception been excessively costly, inefficient and perhaps most of all include many tasks which shouldn't be done at all.

Services provided by local authorities and the Civil Service cost vast amounts of money. Unnecessary services and inefficient ones make us all poorer. They are all funded from taxation in one form or another and use money which could possibly be invested elsewhere in a more effective way. Let us now look at different services and consider whether they are necessary and how costs can be reduced but before we do that let me consider the nature of human behaviour as I see it. Let us first divert a little.

Personal Interest

> *Adam, Adam, Adam Smith listen what I charge you with. Didn't you say in class one day, that selfishness would always pay?*

Professor Stephen Leacock said this of the economist Adam Smith in 1936.

> "It is not from the benevolence of the butcher, the brewer, or the baker, that we expect our dinner, but from their regard to their own interest." Adam Smith 1776.

There are many people who devote their lives to the well-being of others but most of us are selfish. Of course, many Doctors, Teachers, Musicians, Priests etc, are largely motivated by a desire to provide service and support for others but we act in the main, as Adam Smith noticed, in our own interest and that of our family and friends. Except for a small number of people we work for income for ourselves and our family and constantly seek a higher income, more income for less work, a better house, luxury car or more holidays. We also want respect, admiration and power.

If we do not reward people for their efforts many become resentful, angry or envious. Why work hard if you receive the same as those who do not? Why invest if you get no return? Why invent or develop ideas if only others benefit?

We have developed an attitude of disrespect for those who have become rich by their own enterprise, a dislike of companies which make good profits and produce the benefits for investors. We insist on taking from those who are enterprising and work hard and give to those who do not. It is a way of thinking we need to change.

Selfishness, or should I say self-interest, does not only encourage people to work hard, be enterprising and inventive but also encourages some people to take advantage of others. They collect benefits to which they should not be entitled. In letting property, it became evident that many young women with a child, single male parents as well, were claiming benefit when they had a working partner who was deemed to live elsewhere. Many were claiming sick pay when they were not ill and unemployment benefit when they could have worked.

Perhaps worst of all selfishness manifests itself in the very rich committing fraud, false accounting, tax evasion, insider trading and many other similar deceptions which they do at the expense of others when they already have plenty.

The Most Important Groups of People

I have always been told that it is wrong to categorise people. Some people are mean others have no sense of humour, but these characteristics do not apply to a nation or race but will apply to individuals from any country. So, what am I talking about?

Adam Smith wrote about the Wealth of Nations. I think he understood better than anyone I have read about the economic factors which make a society thrive, create wealth and lead to prosperity. The country must have a system giving opportunity to many and encourage enterprise.

I'm going to suggest some arbitrary groups of people and I put them in the order where they most help to build a prosperous community.

The first group, if you wish to make a society rich and prosperous, are the entrepreneurs and inventors. They are the most important people in any country or society. I believe that Sir John Harvey Jones referred to them as the 1 in 200. These are the people who create, run and develop businesses, they innovate and develop inventions. They develop businesses in almost any field, make production and services efficient enabling large numbers of people to have reasonable jobs and live to a good standard and provide the mass of people with the goods and services they need. When they invent or start a new business, they often do not imagine that their business will grow and have a significant impact producing popular goods or services and creating many jobs and wealth.

The second group are the professional and skilled people. We need our doctors and nurses, accountants and teachers as well as our builders, motor mechanics and electricians and all the people who keep the machinery of our society working. People who have knowledge and skills of how things work.

Also, of great importance are those who keep order in our society. Lawyers and judges, armed services, police and allied services, the civil service and local authority administrators.

Also very important is that mass of ordinary working people who work in our shops, factories and offices, who carry us and our goods about and do all those things without which society couldn't continue. We cannot manage without any of these groups of people.

Of course, I haven't mentioned every profession or every job, but all can be placed into one of these groups though some of course will overlap and cannot be easily classified. They all have one thing in common which is that they work and achieve something which our community needs.

In our society also are the young we all must look after, the old people who hopefully have fulfilled their working life and can deservedly retire comfortably. Added to these is a group of people we must also care for who are disabled in some way either mentally or physically and need support. No civilised society should fail any of them.

There is one further group, if group it can be called, for it contains a host of people who contribute little or nothing to the well-being of our society. This group includes those who are constantly drunk or take drugs, those who commit crimes, the group who exploit every aspect of our benefit system, selfishly to take money that should be going to those who have a real need. Together with those who simply won't work. They diminish our society and place a burden of cost on all working people. Many in this group are victims who had a bad start in life, but it is absolutely necessary to hold them responsible for their own actions.

I hope the reader will not protest too much and I agree we should consider all people as equal, but their function will affect the progress and wealth of our community.

Change of Attitude and Thinking

First. We should encourage businesses to be efficient and make good, high profits. We should not expect any business to provide a service for nothing. We should expect the owners or managers of such businesses to be well paid. Generally speaking, well-run efficient companies provide good employment which most people need and they also provide profit for investors, insurance companies and pension funds which any of us can use. They also make the goods and services we all need and which we cannot afford to purchase from abroad.

Second. We have adopted the view that governments and local authorities should provide services. I regularly hear people saying the government should provide this service or that. Local authorities are constantly under pressure to provide services. The more services they provide the more taxation we have to have, and we end up with services costing far more than private enterprise would charge and frequently tasks are undertaken which should not be done at all. We need to remove from local authority services anything which can be done privately.

Third, people must be encouraged to fend for themselves, and support given only to those who can't. From my own experience and observation about 50% of benefit payments are made to people who exploit the benefit system. Sick pay, unemployment benefit, housing and transport are prime examples.

Fourth. We need to simplify our legal and court systems for conveyancing, tenancies, divorce, inheritance and immigration. For example, whenever possible, which should be most of the time, the rules should be standardised and applicable to all and nothing outside the agreed contract considered. Many cases should be handled by an arbiter or judge without appearing in court.

Fifth. National interest should always overrule local issues. It is essential we produce our own food and energy, but free trade is important. If the government undertakes any task, it should be to support our industry and commerce.

Sixth. The old concept of, "let the buyer beware," is a good one. The seller should never have to ensure that a product or service is right for the customer other than following the customers instructions. A retailer selling a coat must be responsible for the coat being a properly made and serviceable garment they should never be expected to determine that it is the right size, colour or type for a customer. That is the customer's responsibility. When someone purchases a property, they must view it for themselves to determine that it is what they want and must use a surveyor to check its structure and condition, a lawyer to ensure that the title is correct, and they must negotiate the price. It is the purchaser's responsibility, and when borrowing money, it is the borrower's responsibility that the terms are what they want.

Seventh. Liability and Compensation. This needs to be reconsidered as it stops some activities being provided and becomes harmful, certainly where people chose to use facilities there should be no compensation. e.g. a children's play area. These can be established and assessed as being a safe design. Unless faults are reported to the owners they should be used at the user's risk and no compensation paid.

Freedom of Speech, Thoughts, Ideas and Actions

Most people have likes and dislikes. People have beliefs, faith and desires making some intolerant. I have often heard it said that if you go to the pub don't discuss religion or politics. What they are really saying is don't talk about anything where there can be different points of view or state opinions which someone may dislike and find offensive or upsetting.

Is it wrong to be a supporter of Manchester United or Manchester City, Glasgow Rangers or Celtic, Liverpool or Everton. I have heard appalling abuse shouted at football matches which is ridiculous. For many years we were friendly with a famous Indian sportsman who I thought was a great ambassador for his country but who was treated contemptuously by some other Indian acquaintances. I never had an explanation, but I suspect he was from the wrong caste which didn't matter to me at all and ought not to matter to anyone.

For many years I campaigned to leave the European Union and a person I've known almost all my life is extremely angry with me and will not discuss my view.

Everyone has heard the silly nonsense about the definition of a woman and how we should refer to and treat transgender people.

I attended a dinner where a well-known Catholic member of the Conservative Party stated that he felt it was acceptable for Catholic schools to discriminate in favour of Roman Catholics. In some fields there is obviously positive discrimination in favour of Afro-Caribbean origin people. Positive discrimination is as wrong as discriminating against groups.

Anti-discrimination laws will never solve the problem. To make progress we need to set an atmosphere of tolerance and understanding and to penalise aggressors only whereby threat or duress harm is done. People should never be penalised for having an opinion or recognising historical truth. We need to plan, by building upon past events and not denying them.

The Welfare of Hungry Children.

I saw recently on television news that a school, I believe it was in the Midlands, had found that 15 to 20% of pupils came to school without breakfast because their families were poor. The headmaster, appalled by this situation, arranged for breakfast to be provided as pupils who are hungry and cold could clearly not study satisfactorily. It is clearly an act of decency, in any civilised Society to ensure that young people are properly fed. Marcus Rashford the Manchester United footballer raised similar concerns about the provision of school lunches.

In a short while almost all the pupils at the school would get their breakfast free or subsidised even though their parents could afford it at home and the same would apply to lunch. The burden of cost would fall on the local authority who obtained their money through council tax, business rates, or general taxation. The desire to supply breakfast and lunch would spread from school to school and the cost would grow, soon to become a billion pounds or more.

There is of course a terrible dilemma. How can we prevent a small number of children being neglected and going hungry. At the same time, we cannot allow the burden of cost on taxation to grow and grow creating more taxation, higher debt and future problems. I think it is the responsibility of parents to care and provide for their children. Do you think I am right? Taking away that responsibility is dangerous.

I know from my own working life that housing benefit is dramatically exploited. It is claimed by tens of thousands who have working partners pretending to live elsewhere. I've said this before.

There are thousands who remain sick, claiming benefit when they could and should be working. Large numbers remain unemployed on welfare when they could and should be working to provide for themselves and their families.

This kind of exploitation applies in every field including our health services where patients fail to attend appointments they've made and routinely re-order drugs they don't use and don't need because they are free aren't they? Someone else is paying. There is a welfare need and there is a welfare greed also. How can we solve these problems because allowing greed and exploitation is damaging our whole well-being?

There is an additional factor which has become evident because of welfare payments. It is resentment. I remember in one of my businesses a young lady was employed part time. She was a single parent with two children and a semi-detached house, presumably with a mortgage. Working 16 hours a week she received family tax credit because of which her take home pay was similar to the two full time clerks working in the office. My two full-time staff were resentful, indeed angry, particularly as she was a quite unpleasant character. I have often heard someone say, "Why should I bother, they get money for nothing."

I believe that those who create and support our welfare system are frequently unaware of this feeling and how it affects the work ethic of our Society.

I believe in our country we have about 1.5 million unemployed, but we have several million more of working age not registered as unemployed and presumably not working. Something in our system is very wrong.

Social and Moral Issues.

I'm very uncertain as to whether I've given this section the correct title. I'm talking about free speech and censorship, hate crime too, and you could add diversity and levelling up. I could introduce the question of diet; you know, sugar and fat, protein, vitamins and fruit and finally let's legislate about cigarettes, alcohol and drugs.

Just about every government I can remember has produced laws about some or all of these matters. I presume they think that governments and members of Parliament know best. My observation is that they take careful advice from experts in the field, debate the subject at length and produce some carefully considered legislation which mostly meets the needs of those who have a vested interest which is then distorted by the courts and ignored by thousands of people who find all the loopholes to make it fail.

The real question is whether we should legislate on these subjects at all. Who has the right to decide what is correct and can it be controlled? How can hating something be a crime? I think falsehood certainly is wrong, but we don't lock up Bishops, Rabbis and Imams who all preach their own faith when they can't all be right. They're probably all wrong but we can't do much about it after thousands of years.

There have been several regulations about sugars and fats but there are now more fat people than ever. We've also introduced several substitutes for sugar, cigarettes and artificial colourings and I wonder whether we will regard that as wise in 50 years' time.

We could of course produce laws completely banning the sale or use of cannabis and cocaine and build prisons to house 20% of the population. Us humans are the product of millions of years of evolution so that we have our likes and dislikes, our feelings and desires, our strengths and weaknesses. Because of this I have my imperfections so I suppose if you were to analyse everything that I've thought, said or written over the last 70 years you would realise that I'm a racist, homophobic, misogynistic, intolerant, overweight bigot and liar- rather like most people. When we go to Rome we don't want to do as Rome does. We want to change their ways to suit us, which isn't liked.

If you are going to make laws in this area, make them simple and unequivocal but perhaps most of all don't make them at all.

CHAPTER 10

Reconsidering The Country's Problems

I LIKE TO REPEAT myself because some things are so important but often, they are ignored because of urgent current difficulties.

"When you are up to your arse in alligators it is sometimes difficult to remember that your task is to drain the swamp."

We all have immediate needs it is impossible to ignore. The problems of the poor and disadvantaged need to be addressed but our long-term problems need to be tackled as well.

Many Labour Party policies, the objectives of which I wholeheartedly support, have led to ever increasing government expenditure and increasing business costs. Government after government has borrowed money to meet these needs, wages have been increased and public services lavishly extended.

This has led to our two main financial problems.

1) The appalling national debt.
2) Our uncontrolled balance of trade with of the world.

The problem of immigration has the same root cause which is the need to support and protect those suffering from discrimination, danger and poverty. This has led to a situation where our population is far too high and unsustainable, and we fail to produce the food and energy we need at the same time adding enormously to our national debt and adverse balance of payments.

Perhaps worst of all are the cultural differences and lack of integration so that we have several distinct communities living apart in the same country with growing friction.

It is vital that we reduce immigration, however unpleasant and harsh this may be to avoid even worse conflict and suffering in the future and to meet the wishes of the British people.

The Solution to Our Problems

- Reduce imports and increase exports to improve the trade balance.
- Avoid increasing our national debt.
- Reduce immigration of unskilled workers which encourages inefficient business and low wages and to reduce our population
- Improve our food and energy security.
- Create a standard of government which puts the people of Britain first and ensures there are opportunities for all.

I would like to draw my readers attention to thoughts I have about our government's approach to the methods and systems we use, and especially the relationship between government and the population.

I have already discussed the question of whether services should be run privately or by the national government or local authorities. It has become customary for government to provide public services funded by taxation. My experience is that much of this is unnecessary, it is sometimes inefficient and adds to the level of taxation required which is harmful. I remember waiting 26 weeks for a phone to be installed on business premises by the nationally run Post Office telephones. You will all recall the massive subsidies paid to the coal and steel industries and many others. I know many of you will hate me for saying so but we have the worst health service in the Western World because it is a state-run service. We need to find another way of providing services without a large proportion of the taxation involvement.

I would like to draw people's attention to the difference between investing and spending, a subject which I have often mentioned, and which is extremely important. Governments and local authorities spend billions of pounds every year because they are under pressure to provide a public service. I wonder how often the councillors or local authority employees ask themselves if the spending is necessary. Could we avoid it? Is this service really vital?

I have personally observed several items which are completely unnecessary, and I am sure there are hundreds more. The constant pressure on councillors and Members of Parliament to provide more and more benefits must be eliminated. It is because of this that public spending is ever increasing necessitating more taxation and borrowing and our ever-increasing debt.

We need to encourage self-sufficiency and personal responsibility whenever possible and dismantle the "Nanny State". You can all hate me yet again because I know from experience that vast amounts, perhaps half of the benefits paid are to people who take advantage rather than have real need. We must deregulate and remove controls, allowing people to trade and operate as they wish. We need to de-professionalise, if that is an acceptable term, enabling services to be provided by whoever wishes to provide them for whoever wishes to use them.

Perhaps above all we need a system for retraining and redirecting people as they need or desire so that education and retraining are always available.

The Government Role

Many times, over the years I hear of the government's concern about what we eat. Too much sugar, too much fat, not enough fruit and vegetables and far too much alcohol. They are concerned about what we say about one another, She is too fat or too thin, he is lazy or perhaps he's a Catholic or Protestant or of this bloody race or that, perhaps not really a woman. They have been sold something that isn't fit for purpose when they chose it for themselves. These are all matters the individual can control for themselves. The insults to those on the receiving end can be treated with disdain. People can look for trouble or ignore it. Don't forget of course that it doesn't matter if you weren't looking where you were going, you're still entitled to compensation, it's never your own fault.

I believe governments concern themselves far too much with personal matters and have created a system to protect people who should be looking after themselves. They should watch where they're going, check what they buy is right for them and accept responsibility for themselves and their family and those they care for. These actions by government cost our country billions of pounds, rarely create fairness and have regularly penalised sensible people to the benefit of stupid ones.

I am responsible for myself and mine you should be for you and yours.

I believe John F Kennedy said. "Ask not what your country can do for you, ask what you can do for your country."

All I hear now is " The Government should, the Council must, we want, they want, spend more on this or that."

Part of our decline is that many have stopped being self-reliant, want more for less, and take instead of giving.

CHAPTER 11

Action that We Need to Take

WE SHOULD DRASTICALLY reduce taxation, reduce dependency on benefits, increase incentives to work, encourage investment, innovation and improve efficiency, improve worker involvement in jobs and improve workplace equality, ensure availability of business finance, deregulate and simplify wherever possible.

There are many others so play your part in making our society better.

Social Welfare
Pensions, Employment pensions

There appears to be almost unlimited variation in workplace or employment pension arrangements. I'm referring to pensions paid on retirement which are established by the organisation by which one is employed and the cost of which is made by contributions from the employer or the employer and employee.

Perhaps worst of all there have been pension funds into which the employer was forced to pay even when the company profitability could not afford it. This has led to several large organisations ceasing to trade. It is never wise to agree to long term commitments as we cannot predict the economic or scientific future.

Employer contributions vary enormously. I have mentioned before that civil service employees have 27% of their salary paid into a pension fund all the which of course is paid from taxation.

Many local authorities pay about 14% of employees' salaries into a fund and many private companies run schemes which pay employees up to 60% of their final salary or average salary as pension.

Over the years many people who had no employment pension were taxed to pay these pensions.

I believe armed service personnel also receive pensions paid entirely from taxation to which they do not make a specific contribution from their pay.

There is also staggering difference in retirement ages and benefits. I know police officers and firemen who have retired at age 50 or even less. Many people are also offered retirement opportunities when organisations wish to reduce staff.

If a system is to be fair, then work pension contributions should be paid for by the employee or by the employer during employment. The present system means that employment pensions are regularly being paid by other people and not by the person receiving the pension. Surely if a system is to be just it should be universally applicable. This would mean that employees in the civil service, local authorities or any other tax funded occupation or service, including police, fire service, armed services etc. should all have the same pension system as private companies. Certainly, no pensions should be paid from general taxation other than the state pension which is available to everyone.

My belief is that at the time of employment the employer, be it a private company, state or local authority should all pay into the employees' pension fund a fixed proportion of salary say 3 to 5%. The employee can add to this whatever they wish. All schemes would be money purchase and run by private organisations, insurance companies or pension funds whose charges would be simply and specifically controlled.

Any employee can retire at whatever age they choose purchasing an annuity with the fund.

Employers, private or public, would not be able to offer additional pensions to terminate staff.

Such a system would be unified and fair for everyone. It would avoid employers being committed to pension promises they cannot uphold; it would mean that people with little or no pension would not be paying for other people's pensions.

I can imagine that civil servants, teachers, police officers and many others including members of Parliament would be opposed to such a system even though it is fair, because they benefit enormously from money paid by others. Clearly the introduction of such a system has many difficulties and could not be introduced instantly but it could be implemented over a period of 20 years, possibly a little less and would in the long term benefit our whole society.

I would be very interested to hear what people think and whether they have any other more workable Solutions.

Pensions, State Pension

After the war, males were granted the old age pension at age 65 and this continued for many years. Originally men lived to an average age of about 70 had 5 years or so of retirement on the state pension. Average age expectancy is now about 80 and state pension costs have increased and become unaffordable.

For women it was even worse as they retired at 60 and lived longer. When suggestions were made to change to the same retirement age as men and to increase them all above 65 endless complaints were made.

It is easy to understand why people need retirement pensions and why people want to retire early but high taxation is damaging to an economy. The age of retirement is now increased to 67 and even this is possibly too young and may have to be increased in the future.

The Labour Party which has always boasted fairness and equality has done almost nothing to rectify the problem. So, what do I suggest is done to make the system fairer, more equal, economically viable, and reduce cost? The basics suggestion which will be cheapest to administer is that all pensions should follow the same system.

The state pension should be a fixed amount for each person, male or female, paid at the same age. There should be no additional separate benefits such as Christmas bonuses or winter fuel allowances. Such needs should be incorporated into the basic pension and the pension should be paid into their bank by the same unified system.

Although we all want retirement pensions paid by the state, that is by the taxpayer, we cannot avoid the fact that we have a massive national debt, and the state pensions contribute to this as they do to higher taxation. There is an immediate need to introduce a system whereby the retirement age is increased beyond age 67. A simple solution would be to increase the pension age by 3 months every 2-years until the retirement age has reached 70 when it would be necessary to review the situation again. I can hear the cries of horror, but we have to cut public spending or our financial problems will continue to grow.

Sick and Disability support

Amongst people I have known have been some suffering for many years from cancer, motor neurone disease, accidents and mental illness rendering them unable to work and provide for themselves or their dependants.

We must have a system to give support to those who are unfortunate in this way, not necessarily to keep them in luxury, but to ensure they have the necessities of life and live comfortably.

At the same time, we should expect working people, when they are fit and well to make provision for sickness or accident which can happen to anybody at any time.

I believe that no sick pay should be made for the first 2 weeks of illness. People should not be paid when they have a day off work whether in the private or public sector. Secondly sick pay should only be at statutory sick pay rate for the first six months whether paid for by the taxpayer or by a private employer.

We are developing an attitude that other people should pay for us whereas we should accept responsibility for ourselves. Such a policy would reduce the cost to both the employer and taxpayer. It would also mean that fewer days would be taken off sick. In some branches of the Civil Service, local authority work and other official employees' sickness had risen to as much as 7.5%, so I am told, which is a massive burden of cost on any business and the taxpayer. Employers, private and public could offer employees a sickness scheme for which the employee would pay to avoid severe distress following long-term sickness.

My granddaughter was inviting several of her old school friends to a small reunion and booked a Friday night dinner at a local hotel. Because they were busy it had to be at 6:30 so she rang her friend who lived 150 miles away to see if she would be able to make it on time after work on Friday.

"Don't worry," said her friend. " I'll log a sick day off."

I found out subsequently that she worked for the local authority, and they could have up to 14 days a year off sick without a doctor's note. All they have to do was ring in and say they were not well and get a day off with pay which enabled her to drive to Cumbria, not do a day's work, but get paid. Is it any wonder our tax is high as many people took all 14 days off every year. How would you describe it? Madness.

Unemployment Support

Our society has, quite rightly, concern for the well-being of disadvantaged people and for those who have encountered unfortunate circumstances. Employment as a source of income, as well as a source of our well-being, is vital. Lifetime employment with one employer was in the past generally available. A farm worker remained a farmworker, a bank worker remained in banking, a clerical worker for a local authority could expect to remain with the authority for a working life.

We now live in in a changing world in which both clerical and physical work changes rapidly, businesses which have existed for many years have to change and frequently cease to exist, clerical workers are replaced with computer services, robots are introduced, and some industries cease to exist altogether.

I doubt we will ever arrive at a time again where jobs do not change rapidly. It has also always been the case that as people get older, they cannot continue to do the jobs for which the physical strength of young people is required. Everybody understands this but we have allowed it to become an immense burden because when changes occur, we fail to adapt and retrain and allow people to remain in long-term unemployment with subsequent benefits and costs.

I have mentioned before the facts that policemen, firemen and others retire after 25 years and of course a 55-year-old policeman cannot chase young criminals, or a 60-year-old man handle heavy equipment in a dangerous fire. It does not mean they should retire at 50 having worked for 30 years and expect to get a pension for 40 years or more, it is ridiculous and must stop. Similarly, when jobs cease in any industry it is not grounds for early retirement but time for retraining to perform other useful tasks. Those who wish to retire early must fund it themselves.

Unemployment pay should be for four to six weeks maximum after which there is compulsory assessment and retraining. Only those who are unable to work because of some illness, physical or mental disability should receive long-term benefit.

In a later section of this book, I propose to suggest a method and procedure by which this can be done and into which I would incorporate other groups of people who need training, reform or support.

Housing Provision, State Run or Private

It is unacceptable that people in Britain should be homeless because they are poor, have experienced difficult, tragic events or are mentally or physically incapable of supporting themselves. There is no question about the harm high taxation does to the financial well-being of a community. At the same time there is the need to provide housing. Our society has developed thinking that governments and local authorities must provide social housing or fund the cost of privately provided services and there is an ever-growing desire to improve the quality of housing and thereby increase the cost which has now become a massive burden on the community.

I ask the question. Is it right that those who do not or will not work for their own well-being should have housing to as good or better standard than those who work to provide a home for themselves and their family and who are taxed to provide houses for others?

I believe, for example that single parents with a child be provided with shared accommodation so that for example two or three mothers could share a house and must work to contribute to the housing costs. After many years of experience letting property, it became evident that many young mothers rented a house, paid for by housing benefit, whilst having a working partner who nominated another address as their residence.

Where a family is working and lives in social housing, they should pay a reasonable rent to cover the cost and no contribution be made from taxation.

The present situation is proving unacceptable to private landlords and the rules are constantly being changed in favour of the tenant. If a tenant damages a property, causes nuisance or fails to pay the rent the landlord almost always experiences a loss because the tenant has no assets.

If the landlord fails to comply there is easy redress against him as he has assets.

The law has made it progressively more difficult for a landlord to evict a tenant and much more expensive, none of the cost of which the landlord is able to recover. It is proposed that the section 21 notice (no reason given) becomes no longer applicable, and the landlord has to give full reasons for the tenants eviction having given proper notice. I wonder if government officials understand why a landlord would wish to evict a tenant. landlords want good tenants who look after the property and pay the rent. They have no reason to evict good tenants and the law should protect landlords from bad tenants.

The section 21 notice should be the only one used, it would free up enormous amounts of court time and costs and would encourage more landlords to let properties. The present situation where everything is weighted in favour of the tenant has discouraged landlords so that almost 50% of private properties have now been sold off and more landlords are selling their rented houses when they become empty. This has made it difficult for tenants to find another house, enormously increased rents and added a burden to taxation. Governments have got this wrong. If you want a service to work well, in whatever field, it must be made favourable for the provider.

Consider the situation whereby a tenant rents a property at £600 per month. There are many properties in the north of England with a market value of approximately £100,000 let at this approximate rent.

The landlord is achieving a gross rent but of £7,200 a year. The landlord must ensure that the property has a gas safety certificate approximately £80 a year, an electrical certificate approximately £300 every 10 years must insure the property approximately £250 a year effectively reducing the annual rent by £360 a year and experience tells me that on average such a property requires £1,000 a year maintenance. Effectively reducing the annual rent to £5,820 a year.

A recent example occurred with a local agent. The tenant missed 1 months' rent and was pursued by the landlord who was ignored. The following month's rent was paid as was the next, but no money was paid off the arrears. The following month was missed again. The tenant promised to pay up the rent but missed the following month, so the tenant is 3 months in arrears. The landlord serves notice on the tenant (2 months) during which time the tenant doesn't pay. Having served proper notice, the landlord then makes application to court for the tenant's eviction. The landlord must pay a court fee of £355 and 3 months later receives from the court notice of possession. During this time the tenant again does not pay the rent and does not vacate the property in accordance with the court instruction. The landlord then has to pay a fee of £75 for the court bailiff and wait a further month to obtain possession. The landlord loses 9 month's rent £5400 plus fees of £430.

This is the situation for a private landlord but there are many thousands of evictions and vastly greater arrears in the public sector where the burden of such costs falls on the taxpayer.

In theory of course the landlord can recover costs from the tenant, but this occurs in very few cases and in most cases, landlords do not even take the matter to court because it increases the costs and is very rarely successful.

We tend to have sympathy for the tenants in the circumstances because they are losing their home. Suppose someone stole £5,830 from you, how would you feel? The effect is the same. The landlord would have to do the eviction work himself. If he used a solicitor, it would cost a further £1000 to £1500.

Is it any wonder landlords are leaving the market, and we have ever higher tax because of those who don't pay.

There is, of course, another side to the story. Is it that the tenant can't pay or won't pay or is it perhaps that there are no affordable properties? I read about new build properties which are considered affordable at a price of £200,000 or £250,000. We should be talking of properties which are available to rent at £50 a week but there aren't any. Should we be building blocks of bed sit rooms with shared cooking facilities? I never hear of them.

No one would propose the idea of going back to debtors' prisons, but no one appears to be thinking of providing cheap basic Living Space. There is a problem to be solved.

Employment Law

As far as I can tell there has always existed a certain degree of conflict between employer and employed.

Those running the business want to pay as little as possible and those employed want better pay and conditions. The trade unions constantly seek for their members, higher pay, shorter working hours, longer holidays with pay, and other benefits such as sickness benefit, health insurance etc.

The employers' objective is to make a profit for investors to develop the business and create wealth for those involved.

Such a conflict was inevitable because of the enormous gap between the wealthy aristocracy, rich businessman and the impoverished employees. Once again, I'm telling you what you already know and it, of course, led to the formation of trade unions and the improvement of workers' rights. I suppose this was the basis of the Labour Party because without combined strength the poor had no chance of improving their lives.

I believe however that many of the battles have been won by employees and I am inclined to criticise the Labour Party for failing to adapt its thinking to the modern world.

We need as far as possible to find a way of avoiding conflict and combining the efforts of employer and employee together for mutual benefit.

The ever-increasing demand of unions for higher pay, restrictive practices and better conditions have made some companies uncompetitive in the international world and businesses have been exported from Britain to countries with cheaper labour less regulation and fewer restrictive practices. We all have heard of companies closing because of the burden of pension costs, high wages and restrictions so that the business has been closed and transferred to other countries. The company I worked for 60 years ago, which was not a British company anyway, but which employed several thousand people in the UK, has almost entirely been moved to China and no longer provides much employment in the UK, which means we have to import from abroad the goods we require.

We are all, as Adam Smith pointed out over 250 years ago, self-interested, each seeking to improve the financial position of themselves and their family. We demand more for the same work or less and often fail to consider the well-being of the business we work for or the community. At the present time, 2023, we have endless strikes including the train drivers and senior medical staff who are already among the highest paid workers in our community.

I am not suggesting for one moment that they are not being less favourably treated and they are certainly worse off than they were. However, increasing their pay increases costs in the UK, increases inflation and makes us less competitive and in the end worse off.

We need to find another way and I am desperately disappointed with the Labour Party, which traditionally represented families like mine, and has not produced a single new idea to tackle the problems of our country and still promotes the system of conflict which, vital for the development of our country years ago, is now destroying our well-being and leading to ever increased debt at home and our appalling balance of trade.

For an economy to succeed industrial and commercial businesses must have priority and support. It is always difficult for people to accept that the businesses must have priority over individual employees and when employees are no longer required or are unsatisfactory a simple method must be in place to end their employment. Support needs to be in place and retraining available to guide them into alternative jobs where the people are needed.

The traditional division between employer and employee needs to be addressed and where possible any conflict reduced. If employer and employee can have the same objective better working relationships will ensue and businesses become more successful.

I believe that several possibilities exist which would include: -

The allocation of shares to employees so that they have an interest in the profitability and long-term success of the company.

Bonus schemes as incentives to employees when reasonable targets are met.

Special rewards to employees who help to improve efficiency.

Representation of employees on the board of directors.

There are of course many opportunities and I hope my readers will think about the subject and produce suggestions which they will put to the political party they support.

We should never underestimate the important role of trade unions, which have given strength to working people and brought about enormous improvements in workers lives. It does not mean that they should demand conditions and pay which harm the business. Opposition to modernisation and the introduction of the latest technology must stop. It will replace some jobs but in the long run will give a business a long-term profitable future and maintain and create jobs and profit. We must become efficient because others will. The needs of 100 years ago are not the same as the needs of today.

I have sensed in the past an understandable anger and hatred of employers who have become extremely rich at the expense of working people, neglecting not only their pay but allowing atrocious conditions of work. I now occasionally however meet members of the Labour Party who give me the impression, as I have said before, that they are more interested in harming the rich employers than benefiting working people.

Employers need workers and employees need good jobs. We need an atmosphere of cooperation not conflict.

CHAPTER 12

Public Services

WE ALL NEED public services as we have already discussed. There are few people who haven't used a bus or train service, particularly the young and the old. Our Society would be in chaos without a police force and our fire service has prevented many a disaster. Just imagine not having a refuse collection service or a sewage system.

I've often heard people complain about planners, I'm at the top of the list as I think many things are done badly by the wrong people and for the wrong reasons, but just imagine how awful it would be if there were no planning restrictions at all. The National Health Service, education and many others are all public services, and we have a tendency to take them for granted, expect them to be constantly improved and free for us to use.

Until about 100 years ago public services were almost all run by private enterprise. The canals and railways were all privately built, landowners-built roads on their land and most people got their water by carrying it from the local well.

Public services have improved enormously which we should all appreciate but they are not free of charge. There is no such thing as a free lunch and there is no such thing as a free public service.

We need to look at the situation carefully because spending public money has led us to a situation where we have monumental national debt and industry damaged by a massive burden of cost. It has also led to a generation expecting public services for which other people are going to pay. We need to look again at how public services are provided because the ever-increasing pressure for more and more public services, provided from taxation, by the government and local authorities, is leading to our economic decline.

The present system has led to the enormous national debt. We need to think of a different way of providing public services without the burden on taxation. At the same time, we need to care, and maintain a quality of life, for those who cannot help themselves.

As my old hero Adam Smith pointed out people are self-centred operating mostly for themselves and their loved ones. People do not like to pay tax and will often try to work for cash payment avoiding income tax and VAT. Many people smuggle bringing goods from abroad which are untaxed wherever possible. Businesses employ accountants to minimise the tax they pay. Many of the richest people have put their capital in trusts to avoid inheritance tax. Many simply fraudulently under-declare their income. I feel the need to keep repeating this.

Equally many take advantage of benefits claiming allowances they ought not to have.

Both groups are wrong, and their actions are harmful to the country. People would not act in this way if taxation was lower, and it was always in the interests of the individual to work for themselves rather than claim any benefit or avoid tax.

The Labour Party has become obsessed with providing services from taxation. The Conservative Party and the Liberals are following suit because they think they will be unelectable if they do not. Their problem is that you can't simply reduce taxes you have to cut public spending and public services require people to pay for the services they use. The government under Rishi Sunak is trying to reduce tax without cutting services and welfare. I don't see any way this can be done. Under them many taxes have increased.

I would ask those of you who, like me, want to see a more equal society where everybody has a fair opportunity, to think how this can be done without the enormous public expenditure and high taxation which has made our country uncompetitive in international trade and built up our massive national debt.

Reducing Public Spending

I have already mentioned several areas where public spending could be reduced to reduce both taxation and government borrowing. Many local authority activities need to be eliminated or simplified, pension contributions simplified and controlled as should the retirement age of state employees, taxation dramatically simplified enabling massive reduction in the civil service.

There are many other areas where enormous savings can be made, and I would ask my readers to think carefully about them and suggest ideas to their political party. Some are as follows.

Public Transport

I recently read that Andy Burnham, the Mayor of Greater Manchester, is bringing under local authority control the transport service. It all sounds very good but what it means is that people will travel around supported by taxation whether it be local council tax, business rates or general taxation.

It will, I have no doubt, be popular with many members of the public, who like to travel cheaply on a system paid for by someone else. State and local authority run services are generally more costly than privately run services because efficiency is not a prime consideration. It costs a great deal of money to provide elderly people, unemployed and those on benefit with bus passes and with the system of compensating the bus service provider. Subsidised bus and train services encourage people to make journeys they do not need to make and to live further away from their place of work. They create a need rather than meet one.

In the end the whole community is worse off and projects like HS2 and even the Manchester Metrolink are sheer madness. If private enterprise doesn't want to undertake a project, it is generally because it is uneconomic. These projects may be nice to have but their true cost is hidden from the individual and in the end make us all worse off.

Public transport should all be privatised and not subsidised. If local government officers want to run a transport system, that is perfectly acceptable, provided they use private assets to establish it and rely on its generated income and not taxation. The assets they currently use are yours and mine. Socialist thinking is that the rich should pay for the poor but inefficient, wasteful services mean that the money cannot be spent on something more productive and beneficial.

Education

The process of education is providing information about a subject or training in a particular subject. This is essentially what the Oxford dictionary gives as a definition. In general, we look upon education as what we provide for our pupils in our schools, colleges and universities.

I can hear the groans of teachers when I say that we spend too much money on our schools, colleges and universities. We seem to have developed an attitude that education is an end in itself, Get some "O"-levels, "A" levels and a degree. Stay at school to 18. Job done.

If I remember correctly, it was the Blair government who wanted to increase the number of people going to university, raising it from about 10% sixty years ago to 50% today and everyone should remain in full-time education at schools until the age of 18.

I now hear that about 1/3 of those going to university, if not more, failed to get a job in the subject for which they have been trained, and if they do, do not earn sufficient money ever to repay the loan or cost of their education. This may be considered education but is time-wasting stupidity and extremely harmful to the country's economy.

What should we expect the education of a young person or re-education to achieve?

I am concerned here with state funded education. What should we expect it to do? what should be the result when a young person has finished at school, college or university?

My view is that we should have prepared the young person for the normal activities of life so that they can read and write reasonably, probably using a computer keyboard rather than a pen, so that they can undertake normal written communication and receive information. Also, that they have a satisfactory use of arithmetic which is needed in ordinary life. Secondly further education should prepare them to earn a living. The second part may involve them learning almost any subject to any level to fulfil an available job.

I have recently heard proposals that English and Maths should be taught to the age of 18 which may be desirable for those in further education but it's not necessary for many. It is probably better for some young people to leave school at 14 and undertake training at work with the use of courses in our colleges where appropriate.

Certainly, the concept of the same system applying to all is costly and foolish. Going to university and ending up with a debt of £30,000 or £40,000 when it does not prepare you for a worthwhile job so that you cannot repay the debt, is harmful to both the individual and the community. Further education loans should all be repayable and only granted for courses where adequately paid jobs are available.

I ask people to think carefully about this and put their recommendations to their member of Parliament.

I would like to address two other aspects of our education system.

Initially, of course, young people should learn a broad spectrum of subjects. This is important and should be used as the basis for assessing the ability and aptitudes of individuals. Too much of education assumes that all people are the same often leading many into training in the wrong field for them. This appears to be ignored in most of our schools. It certainly was years ago and I see little evidence that it has changed.

The second aspect, which seems to be inadequate, is that retraining or further education opportunities should always be available. This is more important now than ever due to the constant development of new processes and ideas which affect our jobs.

Education is clearly important, but state funded courses must prepare young people for self-sufficient lives and worthwhile jobs. It can be improved and save billions of pounds.

Now in 2024 the Labour party is talking of charging VAT on education in private schools. I'm not quite sure what they are attempting to achieve but perhaps they think that going to private school is a privilege and therefore should not occur. What will happen is difficult to assess but probably several pupils will have to leave private education and join the state system so that they received the same standard state service. If more than 20% of the pupils presently attending private schools have to join the state system, it will end up costing the taxpayer more and I feel that is likely to happen.

I haven't heard consideration for the opposite. Why not make all schools private and give all pupils a state voucher to spend at whichever school they choose? Dispense with the national curriculum and allow a variety of different educational systems. We could still have a small percentage of schools run under the existing state system if people prefer that.

If schools can choose their pupils and parents can choose the schools for their children the best run schools will survive and grow, education will improve, and a different type of educational system will exist which is important for some.

In every area of human activity, I have always noticed that where customers have a choice and where suppliers are in competition the best survive and standards improve.

Perhaps we should question why those who can afford it send their children to private schools. Why do some leaders and rich people abroad frequently send their children to British private schools?

I wonder if the policy now proposed by the Labour Party is wise.

Financial Services

At the end of the 19th century in Britain there was still a great deal of poverty. The landowners and businessmen dominated working people whose rights were almost non-existent leading often to homelessness and poverty.

Although we haven't solved some problems those days have gone, and we have a host of benefits, better wages, unemployment pay, sick pay, social housing and medical care, pensions etc. For most people life can now be reasonable, nobody should be homeless, starving or medically neglected. What do I think is wrong? I see that welfare whilst often essential, instead of helping people reduces the quality of life and brings more problems.

Welfare enables a great deal more family break up with single parent mothers and fathers and we have long-term unemployed living uninteresting lives and a burden on the rest of the community. Some people are becoming dependant on the support of others, failing to work for themselves with all the benefits work provides both financial and social.

I've covered these points in a section concerned with financial services because we have produced the most ridiculous financial regulations imaginable.

The concept that the person or business providing a financial service should be responsible for ensuring that the product is the best for the client is ridiculous. It is almost impossible, is extremely costly for the client, frequently prevents the supplier from giving advice at all and leads to compensation which frequently comes from other clients who not only did nothing wrong but didn't even know the transactions were taking place.

Consider for a moment that billions of pounds of compensation were paid to house purchasers because their endowment policy didn't pay off the loan. The reason for this was that the country's economy changed from high interest rates too low and businesses from high profits to low. This meant that the insurance companies could not make the levels of profit they had made previously so that the total payout on the endowment was reduced and not sufficient to pay off the loan. The borrowers had the interest payments on their mortgages significantly reduced from about 6% to 2% for example, a significant benefit, which they spent but then expected the insurance company to make the same profit they had before. The clients in fact have been no worse off and had they paid the money saved, when they paid lower interest, off their mortgage they would have been just as well off. Instead, using the stupidity of the government and the Financial Services Authority, they claimed compensation. Where did the insurance company or bank obtain the money to pay compensation? There was only one place, the other policyholders. Clients of the insurance companies who had identical endowments not linked to a mortgage had their return reduced to compensate the others. This is supposed to be fair.

The same applied to personal protection insurance where innumerable people, who had insisted on taking the insurance, subsequently received compensation. Some were talked into PPI by a bank salesman but in the end, they decided for themselves.

I would suggest my readers study what happened, and I am convinced they will agree with me this legislation is completely wrong.

Millions of pounds are spent each year by financial institutions on financial advisers which are completely unnecessary and in the end places a massive burden of cost on the customers.

Following the passing of the Financial Services Act it became the obligation of every advisor to ensure that the client got best advice. This tended to mean that when recommending a life assurance policy with profits, or a pension, you would recommend the largest most powerful insurance companies. The effect was that Standard Life, Legal and General and a small number of others became the only companies to underwrite any new business. The result was that many of the smaller companies, some of which were efficient and offered unique policies, ceased to trade and about 50 companies became embodied in the Phoenix Insurance Group a non-trading holding company.

I believe this was one of the most harmful actions ever imposed on any industry by government legislation limiting the choice members of the public had and making the policies they already held less profitable. The information about this is all available on the internet.

I personally believe that I lost around £50,000 on my life assurance policies and pension because of the Financial Services Act. Check it all out for yourselves because exact figures are impossible to determine. I am certainly convinced that the financial services act, which was introduced with the best of intentions, has done unimaginable harm to the life and Pensions industry.

We have all heard the saying "let the buyer beware." We use it for everything else and we should use it for financial services.

It is interesting now that we do not expect to pay the bank for handling our money. We expect them to allow us to pay in and draw out for nothing. We go to a cash machine which makes no charge. The reasons why the banks are closing branches is that they are costly, the customers don't want to pay but complain about the lack of service. It should be profitable to every bank to provide you with banking facilities, but they have become political pawns controlled by government and the Bank of England with ever endangered profits and poorer service to the public.

Join me and campaign to free up our financial services, celebrate when they make a profit, expect to pay for the services every business provides and accept responsibility for our own choices and actions.

CHAPTER 13

Health Services

LAST WEEK MY wife's car developed a fault. I rang our local garage we regularly use and spoke to the proprietor. "Drop it in in the morning and I'll have a look at it." he said. I collected the car that evening the repair having been completed.

My eldest son had a much-loved blue Merle Collie dog who had been unwell for a few days. He rang the vet; an appointment was made for the following morning when treatment was provided.

Why should health care not be like this?

I've had over the years very good treatment from the National Health Service, the doctors and surgeons were well trained and skilled the nursing staff excellent but I had to pay privately for my cataract operation or wait 9 months, I'm told that to have my knee replacement the waiting list is 78 weeks, a long time when you're 85, my GP referred me to a consultant 6 months ago, I've just been examined and I've a year to wait for surgery.

When Aneurin Bevan and the Labour government established the National Health Service it was undertaken to ensure that medical services were available to all irrespective of their ability to pay. It is a concept which common decency demands and which I wholeheartedly support. Bevan admitted that he had to pay very high rates to doctors for it to happen. The equivalent rates are not now sustainable from taxation mainly because of the enormous amounts of taxation we spend on other matters in particular welfare.

It is also clear that nationalised industries tend to be inefficient and costly. It becomes clear when you hear the reluctance to make immediate appointments, the provision of limited treatment, that medical staff are reluctantly working for the National Health Service and not for you as a customer. Every business I know is looking for more customers, more trade but not our national health service. Something is very wrong. Neither the Labour party nor the conservatives have proposed any remotely sensible (workable) solution.

The National Health Service is much loved and seen as a bastion of Britishness. I am told it is admired and envied throughout the world so that not one of our political parties has the courage to criticise it let alone make changes. It is assumed that no party would be electable if it failed to support the NHS. It has become our sacred cow.

Not being a politician, I am free to level criticism, which I do, because it is an ideology we can no longer afford and which, because of human nature, is assured to have problems.

Although, as I have already said, I have had some wonderful treatment on the NHS, we now have in the UK amongst the poorest medical services in the industrialised world with amongst the worst survival rates for cancer and heart related illness. I wish I was wrong, but our results are not good. A doctor friend of ours from the United States, when I discussed the situation with him said, "You get what you pay for."

The questions are, why is it not working as it should and what can we do about it? We certainly cannot throw more money at it.

I believe we must do two things, firstly everybody who uses the service, except the most disadvantaged, should pay towards the costs, this now applies in dentistry and ophthalmic services. Also, we should have to pay for each drug used so patients wouldn't obtain repeat prescriptions for something they didn't want. These payments should be in addition to those already paid to the GP, clinic or Hospital. The doctors would then receive additional money so the more work they do the more pay they receive. Patients would not visit the doctor if it wasn't necessary. I would also allow patients to visit any surgery at any time. They would choose the ones they liked best. The survival of the fittest.

I would ensure there is a National Health Service hospital in each major area, and I would allow privately run services to operate alongside these and pay the private hospitals about 85% possibly 90% of the cost to the NHS of medical services. Each private hospital could charge the patient, I prefer the term customer, an additional fee. You would get what you pay for.

I can hear protestations of horror from Labour Party supporters, which is very understandable as private enterprise would be making a profit out of sickness, but we do make profits on our housing, food and clothing which are just as vital if not more important.

My greatest sadness is that I have not heard a single action or solution proposed by the Labour Party who now seem to have completely run out of ideas which desperately disappoints me. The Conservative Party, fearful of becoming unelectable, are reluctant to say or suggest anything.

We can't go on as we are so now that you've heard some of my suggestions why don't you work something out and put it to your member of Parliament or talk at your party conference and get things changed.

How many will suffer or die because of rigid principals or ideology before we change the system.

CHAPTER 14

Other matters to consider.

Honesty, Integrity and Trust

WHY DO YOU think most members of parliament became politicians? Is it because they really thought they could do something for Britain and its people? Are they honest and have high moral standards? Do you really trust them to work for the electorate or are they in it for their own benefit? I believe many are sincere.

When I look back at politicians like Chamberlain and Churchill, I feel that, whether they got their policies right or wrong, they were working for Britain. Attlee and Bevan believed in, and worked wholeheartedly for, the working people of this country. Margaret Thatcher believed she could make the British economy stronger and more secure.

In retrospect they got some things wrong and were not always liked and supported by the people, but they worked with honesty and integrity. They made every effort to do what they promised to do and what they were elected for.

I don't feel the same for the politicians of today.

David Cameron as prime minister realised that under the leadership of Nigel Farage, UKIP, later the Brexit party, was representing a significant proportion of the British people. He clearly thought it was a minority view, that he could hold a referendum on our remaining in Europe, having negotiated a revised relationship, and he could win that referendum with a remain policy and get rid of UKIP and the Brexit party for good.

As I saw it, the great benefit of a European Union was to end the centuries of conflict that had taken place between the European countries with peace and prosperity for all involved.

I had rapidly become disillusioned and campaigned with UKIP to leave for about 20 years. I didn't want to leave Europe but could not accept the conditions of our membership. The free movement of people was unacceptable, there was no reason why one country should contribute more to the financing of the Union than they got back, or that products and services should be standardised where not essential. Perhaps most of all that we could not manipulate our economy where necessary.

I wanted to see a better and fairer society to suit the British people, but, as David Cameron found out, the structure and rules of the European Union could not be changed by negotiation since the power to change and develop our society had gone. Sadly, the only way to change things was to leave.

The people of Britain would not have voted to leave had they been contented with the situation. Our government either didn't know or had reasons for remaining which were different from the popular view. Meeting people from other European countries I realise that their people might also vote to leave but their leaders made sure they don't have the opportunity to choose. The decision of the British people to leave the European Union was not reflected in the members of Parliament. About 80% of is MPs had voted to remain and they acted to make leaving difficult.

At this stage I need to remind you about myself, the writer of this book. I am not a historian or a graduate in politics or a politician but an old, retired member of the public who earned a living by running small businesses and had an interest in politics and the wellbeing of ordinary people in this country and who, purely from a lifetime of experience, has thought about the political systems which work and those which do not. Many of you will disagree with my ideas and suggestions but I hope you will agree that our country has been run, carelessly and selfishly by indifferent leaders for the last 30 or more years with little thought for what is right, with consideration for the future or what the British people wanted.

At least 30 years ago several people began to realise that being a member of the European Union did not make our country more economically sound or secure and at the same time we had lost at least some of the power to direct our laws as we would wish. The parties in government did not appreciate this, or if they did, they ignored it because it suited the large companies which supported the political parties. Many of our manufacturing industries moved abroad to take advantage of cheap labour and we imported cheap goods from overseas giving the short-term illusion of well-being whilst ordinary people were in reality worse off. We have sold our assets and borrowed money to maintain standards. Government after government took no action. Why rock the boat when all we need to do is get into Parliament with all the privileges that go with it, great pension, invites onto the boards of directors, and who knows, membership of that great club at privilege the "House of Lords"?

After the Vote to Leave

David Cameron, Prime Minister at the time of the referendum, who spent millions on a remain campaign and futile re-negotiation which achieved nothing, had the decency to resign when the leave vote triumphed. Theresa May became prime minister, without a real desire to leave the EU, and with a Parliament, 80% of whom wanted to remain and many of whom were determined to make leaving fail however much it harmed the country, so that the wishes of the people would not be upheld.

Mrs May negotiated a deal with the European Union which couldn't be passed in Parliament. Some voted against it as it didn't take us completely out of the EU influence, others voted against simply because they wanted to remain and thought the separation was too great. She called an election, but lacking appeal and leadership, lost seats, subsequently losing her position.

Boris Johnson took over as leader and, as you know, in a short while called an election. The electorate were tired of the stalemate and when he promised to "GET BREXIT DONE" he won a landslide victory. Voters supported him, even "Remainers", because they objected to a parliament which did not honour the referendum or were tired of the stalemate. This ought to be a lesson to Parliament to research the wishes of the electorate and fulfil those wishes. In the previous 20 years of campaigning to leave the EU Boris Johnson was little or not evident. It seemed to me he only adopted the policy to win the election. Many Conservative candidates were hypocrites, like the one in my Cumbria constituency, who believed in remaining in Europe, voted to remain in Europe but stood for the Conservative Party with a policy to "Get Brexit Done".

Is it surprising that parliament and our politicians are not respected when they behave in a hypocritical manner and fail to undertake the wishes of the people. We are still in the European Convention on Human Rights, they have allowed a border to exist between England and Northern Ireland, we have not taken back control of our fisheries, and I'm told over 4000 laws and regulations exist to comply with the European Union. The Conservative party, led by Boris, made the lockdown rules to control Covid and broke the rules themselves. How can anyone respect them? These matters convince me that most members of Parliament are there for their own benefit rather than for the well-being of the country.

The personal behaviour of Boris Johnson showed total disrespect for the public, his successor Liz Truss had policies the Conservative Party voted for but handled them with total incompetence, paving the way for the present prime minister Rishi Sunak with the high tax, high spend policies of the Labour Party. What a mess don't you think? We might as well have a Labour Government.

Labour (and Conservative) governments have continued with policies of high spending and more public ownership. Not a new idea in 50 years. The same old, same old. Leading to the present massive debt and insecurity. We want to have a better, fairer, more equal society but why use the same methods used before which haven't worked? Don't they think? I'm a supporter of working-class people. I want fairness and equality, but labour needs new ideas to achieve this.

About 75% of the population think immigration is too high but this government have allowed, if not encouraged, it to increase. Why would they do the opposite of what the people want? I understand that about 70% of people support assisted dying but it was heavily defeated in parliament last time and at least two of my local MPs will still vote against it next time. Are they, our representatives? They certainly think they know better than the electorate.

The Law on Moral Issues

Many people in our society are obsessed with laws concerning moral or lifestyle issues and we have all sorts of restrictions for moral and religious reasons. Many of the laws which affect individual people such as their right to accept or refuse a blood transfusion, vaccination, or other medical treatment, the right to have an abortion, commit suicide or assisted suicide have proved difficult because of entrenched religious belief. Surely if only one person in the country wants assisted suicide, they have the right. It is not for others to decide.

I do not have a religious belief and I have never been able to find any basis for belief in God and there is strong evidence that the religions which exist have been created by primitive people centuries ago in an attempt to explain a world they couldn't understand, and many religious teachings are now known to be incorrect. Religion however is now so entrenched in human society, often by indoctrination and threats that people really believe them to be true and even state that it is wrong to question the beliefs.

As a person seeking fairness and equality, even though I am extremely anti-religion, I believe everyone must have the right to follow what creed or way of life they choose for themselves. I draw the line at the point where beliefs are inflicted on other people. Many religious people, believing their faith is the word of God, claim rights for themselves but want to deny rights to others.

How much better a society would be if we did not show religious symbols in our attire or in the rules of daily life and avoid discrimination. We spend money to create or ensure diversity indulging in positive discrimination instead of choosing the best person for the task. The government is also talking of levelling up which is a pointless exercise. Business and services should be developed where most suitable. There I go, I've said it before.

Professional Services

In recent years there has been legislation or guidance to ensure that those requiring advice or services are supported by professionally qualified people so that these services will ensure top quality services for people in need. Making sure that professional services of the highest quality are available to everyone sounds an excellent idea. We would certainly not wish to have an operation performed on our body by an incompetent, improperly trained surgeon and we would not wish to enter a legal contract which proved to be invalid because our lawyer didn't know what he was doing. I assume these changes to the law have been designed to protect ordinary people and ensure that wherever possible they get sound professional service and advice. The purpose is to protect untrained members of the public.

I believe we need wherever possible to look at our professional services and simplify our laws and procedures. There seems to be in our society a desire to protect ordinary people. I presume the desire is to protect them from the operations of large companies or societies such as banks or building societies, internet companies or anyone selling a product. We've adopted the view that people cannot look after themselves and are constantly being deceived. The truth is the more people are protected the less they can decide for themselves, the more support people are given the less effort they make themselves.

In effect we create an economy where services become progressively more complicated and costly so that we are all worse off having to use the services of overtrained, expensive people for simple tasks which we should decide and do for ourselves. We need to de-professionalise if that is the correct word, but I hope it will enable you to understand what I mean. For example, it takes several to years train a chiropodist, podiatrist if you prefer, and this is the person we must use to cut our toenails or file our corns which is what about 90% of the public require. Lesser trained people could work with the chiropodist.

In court we must be represented by a qualified solicitor who has spent years of training in every aspect of the law. When collecting a debt, we need a person only trained in the law of indebtedness, when evicting a tenant, the legal representative need only know the law of landlord and Tenant. Whenever possible these matters should be simplified and reduce the cost of training and charges to the public.

We need to simplify our taxation system which would save billions by reducing the cost of of our civil service, the work of accountants and court costs over disputes. Our attempts at fine tuning our systems are the cause of the problem, one or two people have a problem and we create work for thousands. We should avoid altogether systems which affect very few people, and we can manage without.

When purchasing an item or service, it must be fit for purpose and its limitations or risks clearly described so that the customers can decide for themselves and if in doubt can seek advice, but it must always be the purchaser's responsibility. We should always attempt to make our laws simple and concise avoiding obscurity and avoiding legal conflict. Members of Parliament are constantly under pressure to change existing law, often to make it more precise and thereby making it more difficult to follow and leading to greater conflict, delays and cost.

I'm sure every reader will know some wasteful action so put it to your members of Parliament and make sure that those things we do are cost-effective.

Ring-Fenced Laws

A situation which has often worried me is that when our government wishes to do something, take some action to achieve a particular objective that action is contested in a court of law and deemed to be illegal so that it cannot be undertaken. This effectively means that our elected government frequently cannot do what the electorate want.

A second feature is that sometimes most of the electorate want a particular ruling and it is completely ignored by Parliament. The government makes sure that the view can never be expressed, or it is deemed to be illegal and summarily dismissed.

Popular views are regularly ignored and indeed are often viewed with contempt. Surely in a democracy the majority wish must be upheld or we have a dictatorship. Does a government have the right to force its view on the community?

We need a system whereby laws are "Ring-Fenced". This would enable our parliament to pass a ruling, provided it is voted in by a majority in Parliament, without any possibility of it being contested in court or considering ancient laws or other international law. In effect nothing is considered other than this law made in Parliament.

I hope my readers will think about this kind of action and whether anything of this kind is even remotely possible. I know of course it will be completely opposed by our establishment in particular the senior members of our civil service and our senior Law Lords. The government has wanted to introduce various laws about immigration, crime and punishment, fracking etc. but appears to be unable to do so.

Our country is hamstrung by rules established in the past and which it is unable to change. We need to look at this situation carefully.

CHAPTER 15

Religious Matters

Mrs Griffiths, Ivor and God.

THERE WAS A small triangular field next to the house where I lived. It was occupied by a large mild mannered shire horse with the name of Tommy. I believe he was 20 or more years old, had been made redundant by a small grey Ferguson tractor and retired to this small paddock where he was always eager to see people like me especially if I took him an apple, carrot or crust of bread.

I visited Tommy most days after school always taking him something and frequently climbing onto his back to which he made no objection. If you made a double click, he would walk, an instruction he couldn't resist after 18 or 20 years working on the farm.

When I returned with Tommy to the gate a boy about my age was standing on the second rail watching.

"I wish I had a horse," he said.

"He isn't mine," I replied, "He just lives here, he belongs to the farm."

The boy was Ivor Griffiths. Mr and Mrs Griffiths, together with their three children Pamela, Diana and Ivor had come to live in the farm cottage opposite to where I lived, Mr Griffith being the new cowman at the farm. Ivor was the only young boy living within about a mile of my home so inevitably we spent much of our spare time together. We played endless games of cricket and football, spent hours collecting bird's eggs and fishing in the local streams and the nearby river Gowy. Tommy had plenty of exercise with two small passengers aboard.

The Griffiths family we're nice friendly people. In a short while my mother and Mrs Griffiths became close friends and it seemed to me had secretive talks together.

The distance from the farm cottage to our house was quite a long way, some 200 or 300 yds. I remember watching Mrs Griffiths Walk across to see my mother, She was wearing pyjamas, thick woolly socks and carpet slippers. She had on a dressing gown with a large man's overcoat on top. Her long, dull, unkempt hair untidily covered with a head scarf. She walked unsteadily with a stick pausing from time to time to catch her breath.

She disturbed me, making me feel uncomfortable. I thought of her as a wild woman or a witch. I never talked about her to Ivor and from time to time she disappeared for a few days, or a week and Ivor occasionally stayed at my house. Years later I realised that she had been a desperately sick woman and about 9 months after they came to the farm Mrs Griffiths died of what I later learned was breast cancer.

I remember how devastated Ivor and his sisters were at the sheer horror of their loss and how I hated the rector's words of attempted comfort that she had gone to heaven in accordance with God's will. That she was now loved and cared for. Why didn't he care for her before?

People grieve and recover because they have no choice. Pamela who was about 12 or 13 helped by her sister Diana had to look after the house and Mr Griffith worked every day. Ivor and I continued to be friends and life went on.

My mother was waiting for me one day as I got off the bus from school and I was taken immediately to the village to see the doctor who examined me carefully and found nothing wrong. My mother was told that if I showed certain symptoms, I can't remember what they were, I was to be taken immediately to the Royal Infirmary in Chester. Ivor had somehow contracted diphtheria and was seriously ill. He died 2 days later aged eight and a half.

The loving God I had been told about had allowed great horrors to fall on these lovely people. It made no sense to me even at 9 or 10 years old and I never went to Sunday school again. As years went by, I learnt about evolution, genetics and cosmology which illustrated that the stories in the Bible were not correct and I could find no basis for belief in the existence of God.

I am now as certain as I can be that God cannot exist. Most of all I hate the suffering that religion has caused in endless ways and how it has expanded hatred and suffering around the world. How many have been killed in the name of religion, imprisoned or killed for blasphemy, seeking truth or abandoning a faith. The endless conflicts between one religion and another or even between one sect and another. How religion restricts the lives of women, creates misery for homosexual and lesbian people; often enforces marriage and restricts divorce. The suffering caused by religion with the divisive rules of belief. dietary and ceremonial rules are the very foundation of hatred between communities leading to segregation and conflict.

My great concern is that it is as bad, if not worse, today than it has ever been and will lead to greater suffering and conflict in the future.

I would defend everyone's right to follow whatever belief or faith they choose. I wish them well if it gives them comfort and a feeling of well-being. I have met many people of different faiths, Christians, Jews, Muslims, Hindus, Buddhists and non-believers. They have almost all been decent people who simply wanted to live comfortable lives in their own way.

Religious people follow a faith, almost always that of their parents or the community in which they live. They rarely question their faith because that is the road to disbelief. The questions lead to a suspicion that what they are taught may not be true as is the recognition that there are many religions and sects which can't all be correct.

How do I know there is a God? Do people really have a soul? How can we continue to believe when there is no evidence and the world as we know it makes complete sense without one? It seems that most people believe because they are taught to, because they feel it is safer, enjoy the fellowship and the ceremonies. Perhaps most of all they follow, because of fear, fear of hell and damnation but perhaps because their lives, freedom or wellbeing will be threatened by the leaders and priests of the community in which they live.

The human race has made enormous progress in understanding the nature of the universe, scientific and technical progress has made life more prosperous and comfortable for us all but when it comes to religion, we have achieved little, and religion dominates the lives of millions and is the foundation of discrimination and conflict everywhere. Even when the evil of religion is recognised action against it is difficult if not impossible.

What should we do in Britain if anything?

There is a strange pride that we have a multicultural, we really mean multireligious, society but what we have is a series of communities living side by side, not integrating, not trusting one another and having as little contact as possible.

Religious belief, although there is no evidence for the supernatural, is not evil. A person who has faith in a God, whichever one, may get comfort and a feeling of security which is nice. The promise of everlasting life, to someone who has suffered from illness, injury or poverty, is wonderfully comforting irrespective of its being true or not.

Many people live quite happily with delusions which so long as they don't create suffering are acceptable. In any event it is often difficult to be certain of truth.

There appear to be two aspects of religion which cause most of the problems.

Firstly, there are a large number of religions and sects and the followers of each believe their faith is correct and the others wrong. Because they believe their faith comes from God they wish to stand up for their faith, often fighting for it or treating non-followers badly.

The second is because of individual beliefs. I think that many primitive ancient beliefs were incorporated into religion and after time were assumed to be the instructions of God. Men, the stronger of the two sexes fought for their group and dominated everything. I think it probable that when battles took place the men were killed but many of the women would be taken away as slaves or wives. Women were regarded as possessions and remained most of their time in the living place being routinely pregnant with duties of preparing food and clothing as well as caring for children. It is only very recently that women have been allowed a level of equality anywhere and in many countries, they still have few rights.

Marriage, divorce, contraception and abortion are again established as a religious tradition the rules following that established by the religious faith. For centuries they were unchangeable even where it was easily seen to be unsatisfactory, causing suffering and misery for millions.

Circumcision of baby boys and in some cases, girls is clearly an act of assault as the operations are undertaken without the child's consent. Such action has taken place for thousands of years and because it is a religious tradition it must be respected but is still wrong. In many religions dietary laws apply. They have in the past, and still, contribute to division and conflict between sects and different religions. The same applies to religious clothing and symbols which highlight different religious groups supporting segregation and developing dislike.

Of course, if we support freedom of religion, religious people will want to wear whatever symbols or clothing they choose, and it is difficult to prevent this and is I think a human right.

I know however that around the world millions of people wear clothes they would not wish to wear, display symbols, follow dietary rules they do not believe in, and attend ceremonies they do not like but if they do not, they are ostracised, threatened, imprisoned or even killed.

It is clear to any thinking person that there is no basis for belief in God or other supernatural phenomenon which is the basis of all religions. Most people are not allowed to think and are forced by the religious leaders to follow the religious belief with every conceivable threat.

The Church of England and now even the Roman Catholic Church are losing membership because they have lost the power to threaten. Some other faiths are continuing to develop because of threats to life on this earth and damnation in the next. Perhaps there are many who expressed their following of a religion because it is expedient to do so rather than because they believe.

So! What should we in Britain do?

I have noticed that my great grandchildren, who attend a Catholic Primary School, are being taught about the virgin birth of Christ and his subsequent death by crucifixion. At four, five and six years of age they cannot understand virginity and my little great granddaughter was very upset at the idea of someone (Christ) being killed. I know that religious people like to indoctrinate children from a very early age so that they are always subsequently afraid of not believing.

Although it will be opposed by all the religious groups, we should prevent the teaching of religious matters to small children who clearly cannot comprehend. Obviously, parents will have the right to teach children themselves or in their place of worship.

I believe also that we should ensure scientific knowledge and the scientific method are taught to all children at school starting probably at age about eight or nine when they have enough knowledge of words to begin to understand and get a basic feeling of how the world works.

A little later, when they can understand rational thinking, they should be introduced to Darwin's theory of evolution, with all the evidence to support it, and to the modern understanding of the universe, its age, it's process of evolvement, the enormity of its size and power with the evidence of how it will eventually end.

The beliefs expressed by religious leaders of creation and spiritual matters should be compared to this, evidence examined so that children can decide for themselves what they wish to believe considering information provided by religious teachers and the scientific information.

I believe the country should act against any religious instruction which encourages people to break the law. Any religion which treats women with inequality is breaking the law as is any faith which discriminates against other faiths. Action should be taken against any group encouraging or proposing violence against people of another faith or against people who do not wish to follow the customs of a particular religion.

I suggest that the government of Britain should routinely, annually at least, arrange meetings with the leaders of all the main religions to discuss together what can be done to reduce interfaith conflict and discrimination.

I have written a lengthy section concerning religion because I believe this is the greatest danger to humanity, to human well-being, freedom and quality of life. Why is there antisemitism? Why is there a conflict between Israel and the Arab Nations? Why has there been ongoing conflict in Northern Ireland? Why is there hatred between Muslims and Hindus in India? Which country in the Middle East or North Africa offers its citizens freedom of choice, freedom of thought, equality and basic human rights? I don't know of one, correct me if I'm wrong. They are dominated by religious leaders and their restrictive rules.

We've seen the evils of communism in Russia, China, North Korea and Cuba. The Horrors of fascism in Germany, Italy and Spain. These systems have proved themselves unworthy and led to staggering suffering whereby they are unlikely to be resurrected again.

Religion is different and does not depend on the leadership of a Stalin or a Hitler but settles into the minds of ordinary people each of whom believes their faith is the word of God and all the others are wrong, setting the foundation of human restrictions and religious hatred. It is a disease with lots of mutations and there appears to be no cure. It can't be seen or felt or smelled or touched so even though there is no evidence of its existence it is impossible to destroy being settled into the minds of billions in all its different forms. This is the world's great evil. What would you do, anything or nothing? If you want to take action, what and how? Most who believe in their God see their faith as the truth and want to do nothing.

CHAPTER 16

Unemployment, Training and Retraining

WE NEED A properly funded organisation for the training or retraining of people who are or become unemployed and for those who have been long term unemployed. Unemployment benefit should only be paid for a very short period. I personally believe that up to eight weeks is the time needed. At the end of that period benefit would stop unless the person attends a training centre one of which would be established in every main district.

The first task of the centre would be to assess the ability and aptitudes of the unemployed person and assess their mental and physical condition so that they can be directed into a job or trained for one of the jobs which our country needs and for which they are suited.

I believe one of the great weaknesses of our education system, as I mentioned earlier, is that people are taught or trained in areas where there are no jobs often costing a great deal of money and leaving the trained person in debt.

Routinely local businesses should be requested to liaise with their local training centre listing the jobs available and the skills required. Ideally a joint training scheme could be established between the local training college and the employers. This of course could be widened to a county or national level if necessary.

Such an arrangement would I'm sure be beneficial to both employers and job seekers.

Schools, colleges and universities should provide tuition to the required standard when the need for that tuition has already been established. They are appropriate when is has been agreed that someone wants to take a degree in law to become a qualified lawyer, or advanced level French or a course in engineering etc when there are jobs requiring that knowledge. What we should not do is run lengthy expensive courses in subjects where there are no jobs.

We are talking here of assessing people's abilities, recognising their aims and training them for jobs which are currently available. We may also be involved in directing people into low skilled jobs where minimal training is required or to jobs in which they are already skilled.

One possibility, which I personally favour, is to place such organisations under the control of the armed services. The army must deal with people of all abilities assessing both physical and mental aptitudes. They would be informed of the jobs available locally and work with local colleges and universities to direct people into employment. I believe we should consider the system as a sort of Army service and those who find it appealing may remain in the armed services and develop other skills at the same time including the administration of retraining and teaching. Human beings are mostly happiest when they have a job, they enjoy but from my observation our education system assesses people badly if at all and this task should be the initial objective of a retraining establishment.

There are many needs in our society which could be combined with this service. I would suggest many young offenders, particularly with non-violent crime, could pass through this system and people given community service sentences and people convicted of anti-social behaviour. Army discipline and training can make life interesting, satisfying and provide fellowship. It may help many people who feel they are not part of the community and have little hope for the future.

Giving them hope and a worthwhile job will help. It could be linked to the probation service and those requiring support with mental health. It may also be used to recruit people, as I said, into the armed services, help to improve health and fill urgently needed temporary jobs, it could also help to rehabilitate people released from prison.

I think we do the rehabilitation of criminals very badly, but I plead guilty of not knowing enough about it. This would be an opportunity to guide people into a non-criminal way of life and meet our job needs at the same time.

The system needs to be thought out carefully, testing out a few methods in one small area to determine what works best. Think about it and decide what you would suggest and put it to your preferred political party.

Defence and Armed Services

I would like to think that we could cut down on the money spent on defence.

I often hear how concerned people are about the threat from Russia and more often China. They are not democratic countries and past experience indicates that non democratic regimes cannot be trusted. I certainly hope some kind of negotiation can take place between Russia and the Ukraine to resolve the problem there. Tens of thousands have already been killed and injured and nothing achieved.

My personal feeling is that there is a far greater threat from the Middle East, from religious wars and religious terrorism. It was always stressed that dictators like Saddam Hussein, Assad, Gaddafi and others were evil dictators and that, once deposed democracy could thrive in their countries.

Since the removal of Saddam Hussein and Gaddafi we have not seen the rise of democracy, equality and fairness but the intensification of religious run states restricting freedom and human rights.

The conflict between Israel and their neighbours is religious based with intense hatred and fear on both sides. The formation of the state of Israel in what for centuries had been Arab land was always going to be a cause of fear and hatred. The atrocities committed by militant Islam against Jews and other non-Muslims is equally bad each perpetuating hatred of the others with all the misery and killing it creates. The current retaliation by Israel is excessive and will make matters worse and perpetuate hatred and more conflict.

Religious believers, even though there is not the slightest basis for belief in God, treat human life as unimportant and purely as a means of entry to an afterlife for which there is also no basis.

This makes religious people very dangerous and the thought of atomic bombs in the hands of religious people, particularly militant Islamists is terrifying. They would not hesitate to use them even though our life on earth is almost certainly the only one we will ever have, because they believe in the myth of eternal life. They believe suffering and death on earth don't matter. It is unfortunate therefore that I feel we must not only maintain our expenditure on defence but increase it substantially.

The European Union.

The early establishment of the European Union was not something to which I gave much attention. When we went into the European Union, I felt it was little more than a free trade agreement and the cooperation between Britain and the Western European democratic countries. I don't remember anybody envisaging closer political ties with eventually a sort of United States of Europe.

It was certainly seen by the British people as a means of bringing stability and preventing a repetition of the appalling wars which had existed over the centuries in Europe. Nobody wanted more of that, and the EU would prevent it from happening. When Britain joined the

European free trade area in the 1970s it seemed a sound idea, but I must admit I paid little attention as I saw it having little impact on our lives.

It was probably the 1992 Maastricht Treaty which changed everything and should never have been accepted by the British government. Certainly not without a full debate and a vote by the British people not just the government. I believe very few people in the ordinary community imagined the changes it would make.

Although perhaps not stated in words, the objectives of the treaty were to bring all the peoples of Europe closer together leading eventually to complete political Union and a single European state. This doesn't seem to be a bad idea, putting an end to centuries of conflict and hopefully leading to ever greater security and prosperity.

I'm not sure why but a sense of disillusionment, in Britain and many other countries began to appear. Not only did I meet local people who felt this but visitors from Holland, Belgium and Germany who were feeling uneasy.

I remember speaking one morning to a lady who had worked for me for many years and asked how her son was progressing at university. I was told he had finished his second year and doing well.

"He's looking for a summer job. He used to work at a bakery, but he couldn't stand it after 3 days. All the staff are Polish, spoke Polish all the time and ignored him"

The free movement of people was having an impact, and they came eventually in large numbers. This is not surprising as they could earn three or four times as much as in their own country. Many of them worked hard and sent large amounts of money back to their own home. Many British employers welcomed them as a source of cheap labour and over 30 years between 10 and 15 million came to live in Britain. It never, however, solved the labour problem. Some returned home and others moved to better paid jobs creating a need for more low-paid workers. We have too high a population with congested towns, shortage of accommodation and a continuing problem. Allowing cheap labour seems a good idea for some businesses but reduces the drive for efficiency and develops a society where many are poor and must live to a low standard because of low pay.

I also noticed that innumerable regulations were beginning to creep in to meet "EU" requirements. This was part of the plan to standardise products and services to unify Europe. Many products I liked have disappeared or changed which was unnecessary and often disliked.

Perhaps the most significant regulation was that national governments could not finance or support their own Industries as it would distort their competition with other EU companies.

Effectively the British government had limited control over its own economy.

It is factual as well, that some EU countries, Germany, Britain, Holland, etc. paid larger amounts into the budget of the Union than they drew out costing Britain between £300 and £400 billion.

You may remember how Britain was obliged to adhere to the exchange rate mechanism and interest rates rose and rose on black Wednesday so that mortgage interest rates were over 15%. Thousands of houses were repossessed, and tens of thousands of businesses went bankrupt. Totally unjustifiable and unnecessary.

What made me most uncomfortable was a feeling of helplessness, that things were changing in a way I did not like and there was nothing which could be done. Above all there was no political party in our Parliament which represented any of my views.

I campaigned for 20 years to get us out of the EU because I recognised the need to control the movement of population and to enable our government to make any decisions the British people wanted. I can find no benefit in our membership of the EU which has made us financially weaker and dependent on cheap labour. When I ask people why they value the European Union they say it's because it's best but offer no reasons why. If you look at our problems, over population, nation debt and trade deficit together with a discontent with government they strangely coincide with our EU membership and its expansion.

Public or Private Services?

Britain's social and economic circumstances changed after about AD 1900. The law had ensured that estates passed to the eldest male heir. Where new businesses emerged, they were mostly funded by the same wealthy families' descendants. The poor working people were generally uneducated and stuck in an enduring, poor working class.

The emergence of the Labour Party in the UK played a major part in redistributing wealth and improving the rights of employees and the poorer sections of the community.

Labour Party thinking which brought about the main changes in our society has in many people's minds remained unchanged even though many of their objectives have already been achieved and new approaches are now needed. Although I believe in the objectives of a socialist party, I have no longer been able to vote Labour.

There are still many amongst Labour Party supporters who hate rich people including those who have not inherited wealth but developed successful businesses which benefit the whole community, an attitude I really dislike and think harmful.

Experience tells me that many, if not most, wealthy businesspeople provide jobs and opportunities for employees and other working people additionally paying significant tax.

Equally it is evident that many poorer people exploit the welfare system or don't work, to a cost of billions of pounds which should go to those really in need.

Labour Party thinking, which I believe is now partly outdated, is that we must provide more and more public services and more and more welfare.

I now believe that both the Labour Party and the Conservative Party are more interested in being elected than doing anything which is beneficial for the country and our people. I also believe that most people have excellent understanding and will recognise policies which are good for Britain if they could vote for them and have them implemented.

This short book is an attempt to make both the Labour and Conservative parties rethink and change their policies for the benefit of the whole community.

Past experience indicates that if people are given incentives they perform better and if welfare is excessive, they take advantage, work less and harm the country.

I am suggesting big reduction in taxes, to provide welfare only when it is really needed and encourage people to be self-sufficient and run an efficient prosperous and safe country.

The changes I have suggested previously will reduce public spending by around £250 billion a year and we can then make comparable tax cuts. This is allowing for an additional £60 billion spent on improved armed services and training.

My figures are of course a poor estimate and cannot all be achieved in one year, but they show a process we need to follow if we want more prosperous, safer and happier society.

CHAPTER 17

Environmental Issues.

APART FROM ALL the scientific evidence about the increase in atmospheric carbon dioxide it is evident to me at age 85 that there is a change in the climate. I remember well the cold winters and frosts as a boy. Now it is much wetter and little frost. Whether this is all due to human activity or other natural causes is not proven and where I now live was under deep ice 10,000 years ago in an ice age.

I think our governments have made quite an effort to reduce CO2 emissions but we in Britain account for only about 1% of all emissions. We should ensure that every year our emissions are reduced by at least 3 or 4%.

We must recognise however that we cannot allow it to harm our economy because if we do, we will end up less able to continue the task,

Our balance of trade is appalling, and the import of oil and gas is a significant part of it. We must undertake fracking to produce our own fuel, not to increase the use of gas but to replace that which is imported from abroad because we cannot afford to buy expensive gas from other countries and transporting it is environmentally costly.

I believe all new properties and all new industrial and commercial buildings should be roofed with solar panels.

At the same time, I am concerned about the protesters who campaign to stop oil. I agree that we wish to, indeed must, stop using fossil fuels but the protestations are unrealistic and costly to the nation particularly where they disrupt other people's activities. None of the protesters themselves appear to have done anything to help to reduce fossil fuel usage. They do nothing but blame everybody else.

One of the great problems our country has originates from local decision making, we all want to produce renewable energy but don't want wind farms near us, or solar panels in fields or to pay for extra insulation in our own homes.

As individuals we can all contribute, insulate your own home, lower your thermostat, use air travel less, preferably not at all, live near to your work, travel less and shop locally, use a bicycle, cook your own fresh food and grow your own vegetables using household waste to make compost. We can all contribute if we chose.

CHAPTER 18

The final summary of what I believe we need to do.

THE SOCIALIST IDEA of fairness, freedom and equality is just and right. We must support those who cannot, for whatever reason, support themselves. We have all met people of limited mental ability and severe physical handicap who need such support.

What we must not do, which we are now doing, is remove or reduce personal responsibility. Millions take advantage of subsidised public services to which they are not entitled leading to unfairness in our community which demotivates others and causes resentment.

There is a tendency to grant people rights and forget that they have duties too. We all should work and contribute to our countries need, provide for our dependents and provide for our housing, future sickness or old age and not expect others to work and pay for us. We have developed an attitude that welfare is a right for which others will pay. An attitude we must change.

My first concern is with the structure of our government itself. It has, of course, evolved and grown over many centuries so that we have an excessively large House of Commons and a totally unacceptable second chamber, the House of Lords, which is undemocratic and is an inhibitor for change and development. We need to replace the House of Lords with an elected chamber which is purely there to research and review legislation to ensure that it fulfils its intended purpose.

It is also important that we have an opportunity for referenda because there are those subjects which the population find important but about which Governments do not propose to legislate.

The Liberal Party and other small political parties tend to favour proportional representation, but having thought carefully about it, I feel that this leads to weak, ineffective government making change and development slow, if not impossible. Indeed, I really favour simply a two-party state without any of the smaller parties because their issues can be included with the main parties' policies and if a system of referenda is available issues the electorate wish to raise can be investigated and legislation produced.

Local government is again extremely costly and regularly conflicts with the objectives of the national government. In any event, the requirements on most issues are the same across the whole land. My suggestion is therefore that local government should be reduced as much as possible to avoid conflict and excessive cost.

The objectives of the Labour Party which is to support working people and the poor and disadvantaged is an objective which I wholeheartedly support. But the actions of high taxation, nationalisation and excessive public services lead to higher costs, greater taxation and, above all, greater borrowing, creating the appalling national debt. If we don't curb public spending and if we don't reduce the national debt the cost will eventually become so great that our economy will become completely unworkable. I heard on the news that it is to be a requirement to microchip cats. Will this really achieve something worthwhile? Absolutely not. It is an example of actions we should not undertake, one of thousands all of which are costly and an unnecessary burden on society.

The changes I am proposing are enormous and will be subject to great opposition because many people have a vested interest in keeping things the way they are.

I hope that my readers will enjoy this short book and play a part in trying to persuade the political parties to do something to improve matters.

It is my belief that Britain is one of the greatest countries in the world which is why so many people wish to come and live here. I want to make it even stronger and better. A multicultural society sounds ideal but in reality, there are few around the world which work well. This is one reason why I'm opposed to high immigration. Which also leaves us with an overcrowded country which is vulnerable if adverse conditions arrive.

I'm always astonished at how few people become members of political parties, attend political party meetings and express their view. Many of the people involved in political parties and in political activity have a vested interest in trying to achieve what suits them and their associates. Without the attendance of ordinary people at political meetings, this will never change. I would ask you all who read this short book to join one or more of the political parties. and play a part in what happens. From the limited information I have less than one million people are members of a political party, about 1.5% of the population or less. A dangerous and foolish situation.

There is the saying. "The only thing necessary for the triumph of evil is for good men to do nothing". It never applies more so than in politics where so many people have little or no interest because they feel helpless, that matters cannot be changed by them, and that nobody listens to them.

I hope in this book to make ordinary people think as well as to express my view. Think out what you feel will work best, join a party and make things happen.

If we are to have a sound economy, state run services must be kept to a minimum but national control is necessary for essential monopoly services such as water and sewage and the national electricity grid.

Welfare must be drastically reduced, and self-sufficiency restored. Generally, if private business doesn't want to provide a service it is unwise for government to do it.

I am suggesting we cut state spending by about £250 billion a year and reduce tax by a similar amount but this is only a start, and we should eventually reduce tax to about 20% of GDP or less.

Put in place schemes for people to fund their own sickness cover, health insurance, retirement and care. We must only fund those who can't, not those who won't. We must give all the training necessary to get employment, create an atmosphere which encourages business and all the services we need will appear and prosperity will follow.

Give a man a fish and you feed him for a day. teach him how to fish and you feed him for a lifetime.

It is the same with welfare. Give people help and they will need more tomorrow. Make them enthusiastic, teach them a skill, you solve their problems for their lifetime and offer them contentment.

Part of my reason for writing this short book was that, not only was I fearful of our ever-increasing debt, but I was totally dissatisfied with the Conservative government we have had for so long. I never felt that they were competent and really working for Britain and its people and had helped to create this atmosphere of disappointment and distrust.

We have now had a general election producing a labour party with a massive majority and who have the opportunity to put matters right or at least move things in the right direction. Not only do I hope to see a reduction in our debt, an improvement in our balance of trade and drastic control of immigration, but I look forward to seeing improvement in trust and integrity, a reduction in poverty, more better jobs and a safer more secure state.

I feel however that the labour party was not chosen for its policies but gained seats in Parliament because of the rejection of an incompetent, badly led, untrustworthy Conservative Party who's support was split with the Reform party.

I hope Labour will adopt policies for the long-term benefit to Britain and its people and not concentrate on developing a feeling of short-term well-being in order to get re-elected in the future. I'm very sceptical and we will have to wait and see.

Printed and bound by CPI Group (UK) Ltd, Croydon, CR0 4YY